R E V I S E

PSYCHOLOGY FOR GCSE LEVEL

DIANA JACKSON-DWYER

To Bena and Carly, who have responded enthusiastically to conditioning and have trained their owners so well.

CRAIG ROBERTS

This book is for everyone who loves studying the wonders of psychology, plus Jav, Jayney, Julieníque, Martinez, Elle, Graham and of course Wiggy. Naturally, everything I do is for my lovely family.

R E V I S E

PSYCHOLOGY FOR GCSE LEVEL

DIANA JACKSON-DWYER & CRAIG ROBERTS

Psychology Press
Taylor & Francis Group

HOVE AND NEW YORK

Published 2010
by Psychology Press
27 Church Road, Hove, East Sussex BN3 2FA

Simultaneously published in the USA and Canada
by Psychology Press
711 Third Avenue, New York, NY 10017 (8th Floor) UNITED STATES

Psychology Press is an imprint of the Taylor & Francis group, an Informa business

British Library Cataloguing in Publication Data
A catalogue record for this book is available from the British Library

ISBN: 978-1-84872-053-4

Typeset in the UK by RefineCatch Ltd, Bungay, Suffolk
Cover design by Andy Ward

CONTENTS

CONTENTS

PREREPARING FOR THE GCSE EXAM

About your GCSE course

The AQA course consists of two units:

Unit 1: Making sense of other people

The content of this is:

- Memory
- Non-verbal communication
- Development of personality
- Stereotyping, prejudice, discrimination
- Research methods

Unit 2: Understanding other people

The content of this is:

- Learning
- Social influence
- Sex and gender
- Aggression
- Research methods

Structure and content of the AQA examinations

There are two examination papers, one for each unit. Paper 1 and Paper 2 are the same in length and structure: each is worth 50% of the GCSE marks, is 1 hour 30 minutes long and is out of 80 marks in total.

There are five questions and you must answer them all. There are five sections; the first four are the topic areas and the fifth section is Research Methods.

Paper 1	Paper 2	Marks on each section	Suggested time allocation in the exam
Memory	Learning	15 marks	15 min
Non-verbal communication	Social influence	15 marks	15 min
Development of personality	Sex and gender	15 marks	15 min
Stereotyping, prejudice, discrimination	Aggression	15 marks	15 min
Research methods	Research methods	20 marks	20 min
Total		80 marks	80 min (+ 20 min checking time)

Quality of written communication (QWC)

You will be examined on the quality of your writing. This means that, in order to maximise your marks in an exam, you should:

- Make sure that your writing is legible (that it can be read) and that spelling, punctuation and grammar are accurate so that the meaning is clear.
- Organise the information clearly. Try to avoid bullet points where possible and write in full sentences with appropriate use of capital letters and full stops. On the longer answers, paragraph your work.
- Use psychological terms wherever possible and appropriate.
- Do NOT use text language!

	Examples of how NOT to write to gain marks for QWC	Examples of how to write to gain marks for QWC
Writing should be legible	*A definition of aggression in the intention to harm other people.*	A definition of aggression is the intention to harm other people.

Spelling, punctuation and grammar should be correct	Femals have 2X cromasomes and men has XY this is what makes them men and women	Females have XX chromosomes whilst males have XY. These are sex chromosomes, which are responsible for the sex of the individual
Use psychological terms	There's not much room in your immediate memory	Short-term memory has a small capacity, about seven items
	People don't like it if u stand 2 close	People become uncomfortable if their personal space is invaded
	Milgram should not have lied to people	Milgram has been criticised for deceiving the participants

On the exam paper, for some of the longer questions you will be asked to write "in continuous prose". This is an indication that QWC will be assessed in the answer. Be particularly careful to avoid using note form or bullet points in these answers because this will reduce your QWC marks. (In the other answers you probably will not lose marks by using bullet points, but it's a good habit to try to avoid them so that you are not tempted to use them on the answers in which QWC is assessed.)

Revision

Organise yourself

1. Know exactly what you have to learn for each of your exams.
2. Make sure you have notes on everything. There is no choice of questions in the exam, so be aware that you need to know everything.
3. Make a list of what you need to learn. You can tick things off as you go.
4. Look at past papers.
5. Sort out the times you will revise. Try to allow a reasonable length of time but give yourself frequent short breaks. Do about 30 minutes and then take a 5-minute break. Repeat this for three sessions and then take a good break (at least half an hour).
6. Sort out a quiet, comfortable place to revise. If home is too noisy, try the local library.

How to revise

There are many ways to revise – the key is to find a method that suits you.

Suggested revision activities

Write revision notes
Revision notes are brief notes made from your class notes or a textbook. The key is that you reword them (don't just copy), as this means you have to understand what you are writing and this is crucial for remembering. When you write your notes, make them well organised (lots of numbered points) and visually memorable – use different colours and illustrations that might help you to remember.

Summarise the main studies
In an exam you may have to summarise a study in a few lines. Always learn core studies in terms of aim, method, findings, conclusion.

Draw pictures

Whenever possible, draw pictures to illustrate what you are trying to remember. For example, draw labelled storage jars for the multistore model of memory, each jar representing one store and surrounded by pictures that illustrate the characteristics of the store.

Do mind maps

This is a different way of writing revision notes. Mind maps are useful for seeing an overview of a topic; they really do help to summarise the whole topic area and to see how concepts fit together.

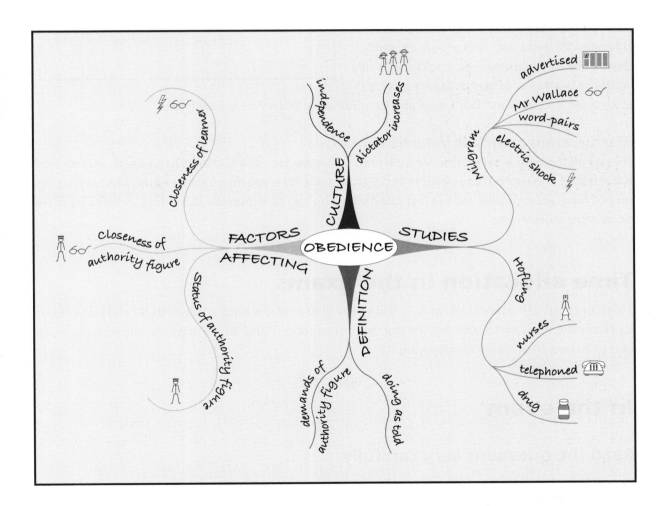

Make revision cards

Write a question or concept on one side and the answer on the other. With respect to methods, you could do three cards for each method (observation, questionnaire and so on), one asking for the definition, one for an advantage and one for a disadvantage.

Do more than just read

Repeat what you've read. Close your eyes and recite what you have just said. Then do it again.

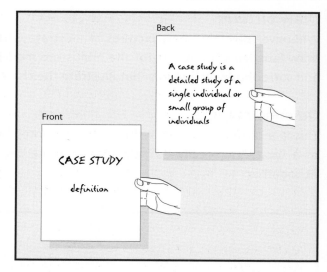

Use memory tricks

Use rhymes, silly associations, etc. The more ridiculous, unusual and distinctive they are, the better the information will stick in your memory. For example, for ethical guidelines (Deception, Consent, Confidentiality, Debriefing, Withdrawal, Protection of participants, use of Children), you could use a silly sentence made up of words starting with D, C, C, D, W, P, C, such as "Donkeys Can Clumsily Dance With Police Constables".

Practise exam questions in timed conditions

First of all, be very aware of how much time you have for each section of the exam and do NOT exceed this. The worst thing you can do in an exam is take too long on the early questions so you do not have enough time for the last questions. This can be especially damaging as the later questions carry more marks.

Time allocation in the exams

Think in terms of *"a mark a minute"*. The exam is 90 minutes long and worth 80 marks, so if you work on the basis of 15 minutes for the first four sections and 20 minutes on research methods, you will have 10 minutes for checking.

In the exam

Read the questions very carefully

Make sure you know what you are being asked to do. Some important points to note are as follows:

- Describing studies: You are used to studies being in terms of aim, method, results, conclusion. You may be asked for only one section (e.g. Outline the findings of . . .). Make sure that's all you write about. If asked to describe a study with the instruction to use continuous prose, make

sure you do NOT use side-headings. Still approach the answer in terms of the sections, but write in sentences and paragraphs.
- If asked to evaluate, do not describe.
- If asked to describe and evaluate (either a theory or a study), be especially careful not to spend all the time you have on describing and do no evaluation, or vice versa.
- If the question gives you an article (a short paragraph on a topic area) or a piece of conversation and asks questions on it, make sure you refer to the article or conversation throughout.
- When answering true/false questions, read the statements very carefully. Many students have thrown away marks by careless reading.
- Questions that start "From your study of psychology" require you to write about *studies* or *theories* you have learnt. Do NOT make up "common sense" reasons from your everyday experience. Use your psychology! For example:

  Question: From your study of psychology outline two reasons why people obey authority. (4)

  Answer: "One reason for obedience was the power of the situation. There is a very strong social expectation that participants will do what the experimenter (authority figure) asks them to do in an experiment, especially as the participants have volunteered and been paid to take part in the study. Another reason why participants obeyed was that they did not feel responsible for what they were doing. They felt that it was the person in authority who was responsible for the action."

    In this answer, note that I have started with a short sentence outlining the reason, followed by an expansion of the point. I have not left it up to the examiner to try to work out the reason.
- Some questions require you to fill in missing words, or draw lines between boxes, etc. Read the instructions carefully and make sure you do what is asked. If you do happen to make a mistake, cross out what you have done very clearly, so the examiner is certain of your final answer.

Look at the mark allocation for each question

This gives you a really strong clue as to how much you should write. If a question is only worth 1 mark you should be very brief. If it is worth 4 marks you obviously need to write more. Think about your answer from the examiner's point of view – have you given enough detail for them to award you all the available marks? If you have not, try to expand your answer, perhaps by giving an example to illustrate what you mean.

What not to do in the exam

GOOD LUCK!

MEMORY

2

What's it about?

Cognitive psychology is all about how internal (mental) processes affect our behaviours and experiences. It focuses on things like memory, perception, language and attention. Behaviours that we may feel are simple do involve complex mental processes. Just finding your way from A to B requires the skills of memory, paying attention and using your perceptual system to understand the world around you!

WHAT'S IN THIS UNIT?

The specification lists the following things that you will need to be able to do for the examination:

- Describe the processes of encoding (input), storage and retrieval (output)
- Describe the multistore, reconstructive and levels of processing explanations of memory
- Describe and evaluate studies to investigate explanations of memory
- Describe explanations and studies of forgetting, including interference, context and brain damage (retrograde and anterograde amnesia)
- Describe and evaluate studies of eyewitness testimony, including Loftus and Palmer (1974) and Bruce and Young (1998)
- Outline practical applications of memory, e.g. memory aids

Key terms

Here is a list of important terms that you should learn in your revision. Try to write definitions for these after reading the chapter, and check your answers in the glossary on pp. 131–136. Essential terms that you *must* know in order to properly understand the topic are marked with an asterisk.

Brain damage	Imagery	Retrieval (output)*
Cue dependency	Long-term memory	Retroactive interference
Decay	Method of loci	Schemas
Displacement	Mind maps	Semantic processing
Duration	Organisation	Sensory buffer
Encoding (input)*	Phonemic processing	Short-term memory
Hierarchies	Proactive interference	Storage*
Hippocampus	Rehearsal	Structural processing

Some important definitions

- **Encoding (input)** means that we create a memory trace when presented with material (this could be visual, sound, smell, etc.). So, it is the taking in of information through our senses.
- **Storage** refers to where we keep the information that we have encoded and then processed in some way (e.g. rehearsed the information). So, it is keeping information that we can then use again if necessary.
- **Retrieval (output)** involves us finding encoded information that we have *stored* in the brain. It means getting information from our memory system that we can then use.

Multistore model of memory

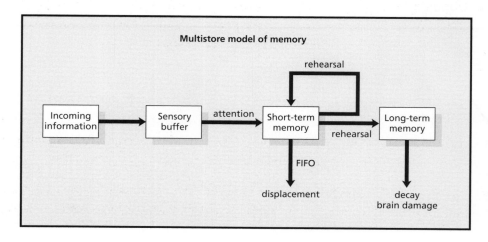

- The **sensory buffer** picks up information from our senses.
- This information is only taken further if we pay *attention* to it.
- If we pay attention to the information then it can enter our **short-term memory (STM)**. This has a limited capacity – it is believed that it can hold seven plus or minus two items of information. These memories last from 15 to 30 seconds.
- Once the amount of information goes above the maximum amount that can fit into our STM something happens – the item that was first into your STM will be the first out (FIFO, First In First Out)!
- If we **rehearse/repeat** the information then it could go into **long-term memory**. Here it can be stored indefinitely and potentially lasts forever as capacity here is unlimited.
- **Decay** can happen, whereby information simply gets more and more faint, or **brain damage**, where the memories that were physically stored in the brain are literally removed or damaged.

First in, first out!

EVALUATION

⊕ There is some supporting evidence for the limited capacity of short-term memory (Glanzer & Cunitz, 1966; see pp. 13 in this revision guide).

⊕ Case studies of brain-damaged patients can lend support to there being separate short-term and long-term memory stores (see p. 16 of this revision guide for examples).

> ⊘ Atkinson and Shiffrin may have been incorrect about the potential capacity of short-term memory (Boutla et al., 2004; see p. 219 of *Psychology for GCSE Level, 2nd Edition*).
>
> ⊘ The multistore model cannot explain how some distinctive information gets into long-term memory without going through the processes highlighted in it.

Reconstructive theory of memory

As the name of the theory suggests, we may reconstruct what we *think* we saw or processed to help us retrieve it from long-term memory.

Examples

- Bartlett (1932) proposed the idea of reconstruction. When we retrieve stored information it is influenced by the attitudes and feelings we felt at the time we processed it. Therefore, we actively reconstruct our memories from a range of information. The reason this could happen is due to **schemas** (pockets of memory that hold information about a particular thing; for example we can all visualise a cat or a tree, and we are activating our schema of those when we think) – see his example on p. 14 of this revision guide. Schemas do change over time, depending on our experiences with the world. We adapt schemas and we also create new ones as we encounter new objects, people, etc.
- Another example comes from Allport and Postman (1947). Participants were shown a picture of a scruffy white man holding a razor and arguing with a black man in a suit. Participants had to recall the picture to the next participant, and so on. By the end, the descriptions had changed so much that it was claimed that the black man was holding the razor!

"Levels of processing" theory of memory

Craik and Lockhart (1974) stated that long-term memories are a by-product of the way in which we process information. They proposed three different levels of processing:

1. **Structural**. This refers to processing things in relation to the way they look (e.g. the structure of things).
2. **Phonemic/phonetic**. This refers to processing things in relation to how they sound.
3. **Semantic**. This refers to processing things in relation to what they mean.

An example to help you!

- *Structural*: Is the following word in UPPER CASE? waffle
- *Phonemic*: Does the following word rhyme with water? daughter
- *Semantic*: Does the following word fit into the sentence "_____ is a type of fruit"? banjo

Studies that investigate explanations of memory

Multistore model of memory

STUDY: GLANZER AND CUNITZ (1966)

Aim: To test out whether short-term memory has a limited capacity.

Method: A total of 46 army-enlisted men took part in this experiment. They were shown words projected onto a screen every 3 seconds. The word list consisted of 15 words. Either:

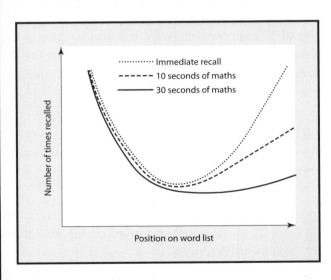

1. The participant was allowed to recall as many words as possible straightaway.
2. The participant had to begin counting for 10 seconds and then was allowed to recall as many words as possible.
3. The participant had to begin counting for 30 seconds and then was allowed to recall as many words as possible.

Results: The results are plotted on the graph.

Conclusion: It would appear that the results support the idea of short-term memory having a limited capacity. The participants in the third group had undergone displacement via FIFO (First In First Out) and all that was left in their short-term memory was numbers, hence they could not recall any of the words from the end of the list.

Reconstructive theory of memory

STUDY: BARTLETT (1932)

Aim: To test out the idea of reconstructive memories.

Method: Bartlett tested this out by getting participants to read a passage of information and then pass that information on to the next person, who passed it on to the next person and so on. He used a Native American story called "War of the Ghosts".

Results: After the story had been passed on through six people it had changed in many ways. It was much shorter (usually less than half the original length). Also, the details that were left out were about Native American culture, so the story sounded more like an English one.

Conclusion: The reason why this could happen is due to schemas (pockets of memory that hold information about a particular thing), therefore when we are reconstructing we activate these schemas and make use of them.

"Levels of processing" theory of memory

STUDY: CRAIK AND TULVING (1975)

Aim: To test the levels of processing theory of memory proposed by Craik and Lockhart.

Method: Craik and Tulving ran a series of 10 experiments (we are going to look at Experiment 2). A series of questions were posed to the participants (as highlighted below) – 20 for each level of processing, with 10 *yes* answers and 10 *no* answers. After each question the participant looked into a *tachistoscope*, where a word was presented for 200 ms. They then responded with a *yes* or *no*. After this particular task, the 24 participants were given a typed list of 180 words (60 they had seen and 120 distractors). They had to choose which ones they *recognised* from the tachistoscope. All words were five-letter common concrete nouns.

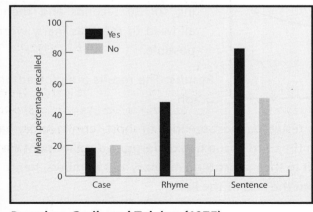

Based on Craik and Tulving (1975)

Examples of questions were:

1. Is the word in capital letters? table
2. Does the word rhyme with shower? grass
3. Is the word a type of fruit? apple

Results: The bar chart shows the percentage of words recognised.

Conclusion: The findings do support levels of processing.

Interference and forgetting

- **Proactive interference**. This is when information that you have already processed interferes with new information you are trying to process, with the end result that you forget the new information.
- **Retroactive interference**. This is when new learning interferes with material that you have already previously processed and stored.

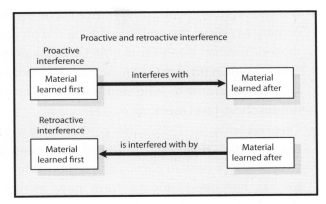

Context and forgetting

This theory proposes that we forget information because there is a *mismatch* in cues at encoding and retrieval. There are two types of cue dependency:

1. *Context dependent*. This refers to cues that are external to us.
2. *State dependent*. This refers to cues that are internal to us.

STUDY: GODDEN AND BADDELEY (1975)

Aim: To test out whether we need cues to help us recall information.

Method: A total of 18 participants attempted to remember a word list consisting of 36, unrelated, different words. The participants were split into four different conditions: dry–dry; dry–wet; wet–dry; wet–wet. There was a 4-minute gap between seeing the words and being able to recall them. Then, all participants were given 2 minutes to recall as many words as possible.

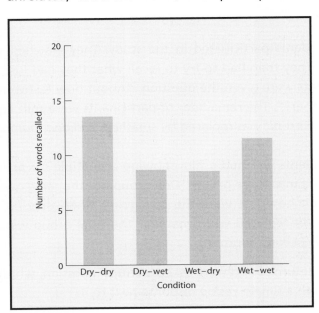

Results: The results are shown in the graph.

Conclusion: As can clearly be seen, the participants who had a mismatch in cues at encoding and retrieval were more likely to forget words from the list.

Brain damage and forgetting

- *HM* was a patient who suffered from severe epilepsy. When he was 27 years old he underwent surgery to relieve the epilepsy. During the procedure, large parts of his temporal lobes were removed. This had a very large effect on his memory systems. He could handle the seven items of information in his short-term memory but could not then get the information into his rehearsal loop to transfer it to long-term memory. Therefore his long-term memory was damaged but not his short-term memory.

- *Clive Wearing*. In 1985, Clive contracted a virus that normally causes cold sores (a type of herpes virus). However, instead of it forming a cold sore it attacked his brain (around the temporal lobes and in particular a region called the *hippocampus*), causing damage. Since then he has not been able to form new memories. The area of the brain that had been damaged meant he could not transfer information to long-term memory. As a result of this, it has been argued that he basically restarts his memory system every 18 seconds (the length of time his short-term memory lasts for). He only remembers fragments of his life prior to 1985.

Studies into eyewitness testimony

STUDY: LOFTUS AND PALMER (1974)

Aim: The researchers wanted to investigate whether language could affect memory of a car crash.

Method:

- *Experiment 1*. A total of 45 students participated in the study. They watched seven films depicting traffic accidents. They then had to try to recall what they had just seen. The first group of nine participants were given the question: "About how fast were the cars going when they *hit* each other?". The remainder of participants were split equally into four other groups and the word *hit* was replaced by *smashed, collided, bumped* or *contacted*.

- *Experiment 2*. This time, 150 students watched a film showing a multiple car accident. The participants were actually split into three groups. One group got the same question as those in Experiment 1: "About how fast were the cars going when they *hit* each other?". The second group had *hit* replaced with *smashed*. The final group were not asked about the speed of the cars (a control group).

One week later all the participants returned and were asked a critical question, which was "*Did you see any broken glass?*", with a simple yes/no response next to it.

Results:

- *Experiment 1*

Mean responses to the question "About how fast were the cars going when they *hit* each other?"				
Verb condition				
Smashed	**Collided**	**Bumped**	**Hit**	**Contacted**
40.8 mph	39.3 mph	38.1 mph	34.0 mph	31.8 mph

- *Experiment 2*

Distribution of *Yes* and *No* responses to the question "Did you see any broken glass?"			
	Verb condition		
Response	**Smashed**	**Hit**	**Control**
Yes	16	7	6
No	34	43	44

Conclusion:

- *Experiment 1.* It would appear that the verbs used in questions may affect people's perception of a car accident.
- *Experiment 2.* It would appear that the wording of questions again can cause participants to report things that they never saw.

EVALUATION

➕ As the study is well controlled, Loftus and Palmer can be confident that it was the independent variables in both studies that were affecting eyewitness recall.

➕ One of the studies had a large sample size, meaning that it is *more likely* to generalise to the target population.

➖ However, both studies used students who may have a superior memory system to other types of people because they are at university and are used to remembering information.

➖ The studies may lack ecological validity in two ways: in a laboratory and watching the event as a film, both of which are not like real life.

STUDY: BRUCE AND YOUNG (1998) – STUDY BY BURTON ET AL.

Aim: To examine the ability of participants to identify faces from video security devices.

Method: Sixty participants were recruited for the study (20 students who had been taught by the people in the videos; 20 students from other departments; 20 police officers). They were tested individually in an experimental room where they watched 10 video clips of university staff entering buildings. They watched each clip twice after which they were shown high-quality pictures of people's faces and had to rate each one. They were shown faces of people who had appeared but also faces of people who had not (seen and unseen).

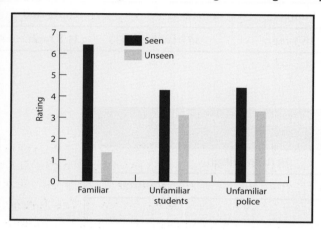

Results: The results are shown in the bar chart.

Conclusion: Familiarity with the target on the video clip had a large effect on identification.

EVALUATION

➕ As the study is well controlled, Burton et al. can be confident that it was familiarity that affected the ratings given for each picture.

➖ A small sample size could make it difficult to generalise beyond the sample used, as there were only 20 in each group.

➖ The rating system is subjective, so a rating of 5 according to one participant may not be a 5 according to another participant.

Memory aids

PRACTICAL APPLICATIONS OF RESEARCH INTO MEMORY: MEMORY AIDS

Hierarchies   Mind maps   Imagery   Method of loci

Hierarchies

With this technique, material that you wish to learn is placed into a hierarchy. The hierarchy begins with something general and the further down the hierarchy you go, the more specific the information is. You may wish to try this with a topic of your choice.

Evidence

Bower, Clark, Lesgold and Winzenz (1969) asked people to learn words that had been placed into a hierarchy diagram or not. For those in the organised group, their average recall was 73 words. For the random group, their recall averaged only 21.

Mind maps

According to Buzan (2005), "a Mind Map is the easiest way to put information into your brain and take information out of the brain" (p. 6). He compares mind maps to the map of a city. The centre of a mind map is like the centre of a city, as it represents the main idea. The main roads out of the city represent the main areas of information we are wishing to learn. The further out of the city we go, the more roads appear and this represents more information and thoughts. An example of a mind map can be seen on p. 5 of this revision guide.

Imagery and memory

One way that we can use *imagery* to help us to recall information is to visualise images of the material.

Evidence

Bower and Winzenz (1970) gave participants word pairs to learn. Group 1 participants were simply told to repeat the pairs several times. Group 2 participants were asked to construct a mental picture of the two words interacting. The latter group recalled over twice as many word pairs as the first group.

Wollen, Weber and Lowry (1972) wanted to see if bizarreness in imagery helped us to recall word pairs. Participants were split into four groups:

1. Images interacting and bizarre.
2. Images interacting but not bizarre.
3. Images not interacting but bizarre.
4. Images not interacting and not bizarre.

Interestingly, if the images were interacting, recall improved. Bizarreness did not improve recall any further.

Method of loci

Bower (1970) highlighted the steps that should be used in this technique:

1. Memorise a list of locations that are already arranged in a logical order. A good example could be your route to school, college or workplace.
2. Create an image for each item of information that you wish to remember.
3. Take these items in the order that you feel they need to be learned and associate them in turn with locations you have chosen.

Evidence

Groninger (1971) tested out the method of loci with a list of 25 words. Group 1 participants were asked to use a familiar route and place the 25 words along it. Group 2 were simply asked to try to remember the 25 words in any way they liked. At both 1 and 5 weeks after the learning phase, Group 1 (the method of loci group) recalled more words.

OVER TO YOU

Now try the following revision activities:

1. Using *any one* of the memory aids, take an area (e.g. theories of memory) and create a mind map, use imagery, etc.
2. For each of the studies you need to know, type up all the sentences separately for aim, all the bits of the procedure and results plus the conclusion. Cut out each sentence and muddle them *all* together for *all* studies and try to put them *all* back in order! Good luck!

EXAMPLE EXAM QUESTIONS

1 Describe what is meant by the term *encoding*. Use an example in your answer. **3 MARKS**

2 Describe the "levels of processing" theory of memory. **4 MARKS**

3 Outline how brain damage may affect our memory. You may wish to use case studies in your answer. **5 MARKS**

4 Evaluate the Bruce and Young (1998) study into face perception. **4 MARKS**

MODEL ANSWER TO QUESTION 4

The sample size was quite small with only 20 participants in each group. This may make it difficult to generalise to the general public, as there was not a cross-section used in the study. Also, as there were only 20 in each group, participant variables could have got in the way – that is, it might not have been familiarity affecting the ratings but something else. The rating system is subjective and so it may be difficult to compare each participant's response: a rating of 5 according to one participant may not be a 5 according to another participant.

NON-VERBAL COMMUNICATION

3

What's it about?

Communication is essential to survival. In humans it is a very important part of their social behaviour and they spend a great deal of time communicating with each other. An essential means of communication between people is verbal, that is, it involves speech and can also involve writing since this stands for language. But an additional and very important means of communicating is not by what we say but what we do. Even during speech, a great deal of information is conveyed by the *way* in which we speak (the fact that I need to use italics for emphasis makes this point). The tone of our voice, the gestures we use and our facial expressions all convey meaning. In this chapter we look at some of the non-verbal means by which we communicate: eye contact, facial expression, the way we stand, the distance we keep between people. We also look at cultural, individual and sex differences in the way these communication systems are used.

WHAT'S IN THIS UNIT?

The specification lists the following things that you will need to be able to do for the examination:

- Distinguish between non-verbal and verbal communication, including paralinguistics
- Describe types of non-verbal communication, including: functions of eye contact (Argyle, 1975); facial expressions and the hemispheres of the brain (Sackeim, 1978); body language; posture, gestures and touch
- Describe and evaluate studies of non-verbal communication and verbal communication (including Argyle, Alkema & Gilmore, 1971)
- Understand what is meant by personal space and the factors that affect it (cultural norms, sex differences, individual differences, status) and describe and evaluate studies of personal space
- Understand contemporary implications of studies of non-verbal communication and their benefits and drawbacks

Key terms

Here is a list of important terms that you should learn in your revision. Try to write definitions for these after reading the chapter, and check your answers in the glossary on pp. 131–136. Essential terms that you *must* know in order to properly understand the topic are marked with an asterisk.

Body language*	**Non-verbal**	**Postural echo***
Cultural norms	**communication***	**Sex differences**
Eye contact	**Paralanguage**	**Status**
Facial expression	**Paralinguistics***	**Verbal communication***
Individual differences	**Personal space***	

Definitions

- **Verbal communication** is communication that involves speech or is in written form.
- **Non-verbal communication (NVC)** involves messages expressed by communication other than linguistic means, that is, communication that does not use words. This includes the expression in the voice, gestures and body language.

Non-verbal communication can be divided into two types:

- Communication during speech, such as the tone of voice, the pausing, the "hums and haws" and the general pace of the speech.
- Communication that does not involve any speech at all, such as our posture or facial expression.

Communication during speech: Paralinguistics

Paralinguistics is the study of **paralanguage**, which in turn refers to *the non-verbal elements of communication that express emotion and the meaning of the message*. This includes the pitch of the voice, the urgency of expression, the speed of talking. Paralinguistics is the study of *how* something is said, whilst linguistics is concerned with *what* is said.

Important paralinguistics	
Type of paralinguistic	**What it may indicate**
Tone of voice	This can be used to show anger, love, sympathy, humiliation, irritation
Speed	Speaking quickly may indicate anxiety, whilst talking slowly may indicate a relaxed manner or boredom
Pitch	High-pitched voice indicates panic, upset or anxiety
Pauses	Lots of pauses may indicate a lack of confidence, whilst few pauses indicates the opposite

Researching paralinguistics

"Content-free" speech – speech that has been electronically modified so the words are unintelligible – has been used to investigate the power of paralinguistics. It has been found that people are quite capable of picking up the emotion being expressed and the strength of it (Starkweather, 1961). Paralinguistic cues are more influential than verbal ones; if there is a contradiction between what is said and the way it is said, then people take more notice of the paralinguistics than they do of the words themselves.

Communication that does not involve speech

This includes:

- Eye contact
- Facial expression
- Body language
- Touch
- Personal space (the distance people keep between themselves and others)

Eye contact

Functions of eye contact

It provides feedback to others on our mood and personality

- Moods: A high level of eye contact or gaze implies interest, intimacy, attraction or respect. A low level indicates embarrassment, shame or disinterest.

- Personality: People who make frequent eye contact are judged as honest, straightforward, friendly and likeable (Kleinke et al., 1974). People who avoid eye contact are seen as unfriendly, shifty or shy (Zimbardo, 1977). See the study by Exline et al. (1967) below and on p. 103 of *Psychology for GCSE Level, 2nd Edition*.

It regulates the flow of conversation

- When we have a conversation with someone we look at them intermittently: we make eye contact in bursts of about 3 seconds and then look away.
- Turn taking: Eye contact helps to show when the talker wants to carry on speaking and when they want to stop. People tend to look more at the end of what we are saying but look away at the start, especially if they are answering a question (Kendon, 1967).
- Feedback: At the beginning of what they are saying people do not need a response, but towards the end of it they use eye contact to see how the conversation has been received.

It provides additional meaning

- An "eyeflash" (looking at the person directly and then looking away again quickly) is used to emphasise a point.
- Ordinary glances are used to emphasise particular words or phrases.
- A glance by the speaker in the direction of someone else can indicate who they want to speak next.

It expresses emotion

Pupil dilation expresses excitement, interest or fear. Hess et al. (1960) measured the pupil size of men and women whilst they viewed certain pictures and found that men's pupils enlarged by about 18% when they viewed a picture of a naked woman, whilst a woman's pupils enlarged by about 20% when she saw an image of a naked man. Subconsciously we take in this information and are affected by it – without a word being said, people know if someone is interested in them and they respond accordingly.

STUDY: EXLINE ET AL. (1967)

Aim: To assess the effect of different amounts of eye contact on people's judgement of others.

Method: Confederates (people who worked for the researcher) interviewed the participants one at a time. During the interview they were asked to make eye contact either 15% of the time or 80% of the time. The participants were then asked to describe their interviewer, using a checklist of words.

Results:

- Confederates who made eye contact only 15% of the time were described as cold, defensive, immature and submissive.
- Confederates who made eye contact 80% of the time were described as friendly, self-confident, natural, mature and sincere.

Conclusion: The amount of eye contact can have a significant effect on how others are judged. If you want to make a positive impression on someone, you should maintain a high level of eye contact.

EVALUATION

➕ *The findings are significant, with useful application*: They demonstrate how differently we are likely to judge people who make different amounts of eye contact and how negatively people are viewed when they make very little eye contact. It therefore has useful applications.

➖ *Lack of ecological validity*: This study uses rather an artificial situation with a deliberate attempt to use a certain amount of eye contact, so it cannot totally reflect how people behave in ordinary conversations.

Facial expression

Ekman et al. (1976) demonstrated that it is innate for people to recognise and be able to express the following "universal" emotions by facial expression:

- Surprise
- Fear
- Anger
- Disgust
- Happiness
- Sadness

The development of understanding of facial expression

- 3–5 months old: Infants can discriminate first joy, then surprise, fear and sadness.
- 2 years old: Children can recognise all six main facial expressions for emotion.

- 6 years old: Children can begin to tell if the face and inner emotion do not match – in other words, they can tell that a sad person who is smiling is not really happy.

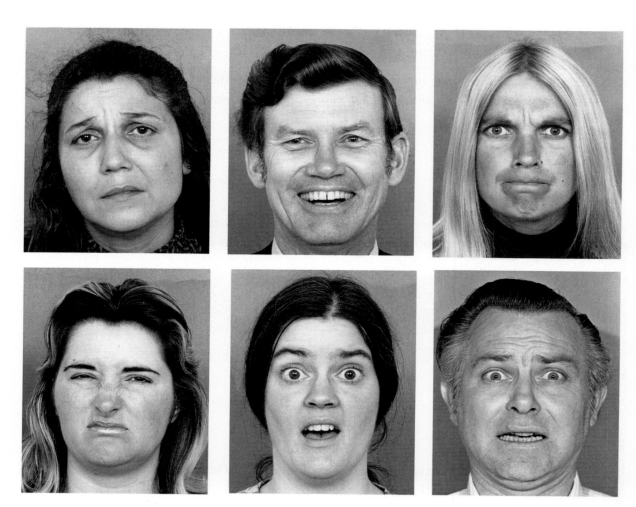

Copyright © Paul Ekman

Facial expression and the brain

Research on the brain indicates that each "half", or hemisphere as it is known, has a different set of functions (although there is a lot of overlap). The left half, for example, is responsible for language. The right side has been associated with more "primitive" processes such as emotion. Since the right side of the brain controls the left side of the face, and vice versa, one way in which it is possible to explore this idea is to see whether the left side of the face is more emotionally expressive than the other. This is investigated in the following study.

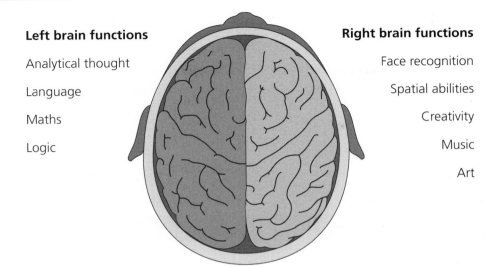

Left brain functions

Analytical thought

Language

Maths

Logic

Right brain functions

Face recognition

Spatial abilities

Creativity

Music

Art

STUDY: SACKEIM ET AL. (1978)

Aim: To see whether one side of the face is more expressive than the other and to infer from this whether one side of the brain is more involved in emotion than the other.

Method: The researchers photographed faces showing a variety of different emotions. They then cut the photos down the middle, through the nose, and reproduced a mirror image of each side. Such faces are known as *composites*. They then asked people to judge the intensity with which each face expressed emotion.

Results: The left side composite faces were judged as expressing a far more intense emotion than the right side composites. The researchers concluded that "emotions are expressed more intensely on the left side of the face".

Conclusion: Since the left hand side of the face is controlled mainly by the right hemisphere of the brain, and it is this side of the face that is more emotionally expressive, it seems likely that basic emotions are controlled by the *right* hemisphere of the brain.

EVALUATION

- *Findings appear valid*: Other research has shown that the right hemisphere of the brain is largely responsible for basic emotions, which indicates that the findings are valid (they are true).

- *The methodology was quite ingenious*: The use of composite faces enabled one side of the face to be judged independently of the other. If a proper face had been used and each half covered up in turn, it would have been quite artificial because we don't look at half-faces when we judge emotions.

○ *The study lacks ecological validity*: The photos used were posed, not taken when people were showing true emotions, so they may not reflect how emotions are expressed in everyday life. The only emotion that was spontaneously shown during the photo-shoot was happiness, and with this one there was no difference in the intensity of the left and right side composites.

Body language

Posture

Posture	Meaning
Hunched shoulders with head down	Lack of confidence
Shoulders back with head held high	Self-confidence; authority
Relaxed posture	"At home" feeling; lack of anxiety
Orientation of body towards a person, especially if leaning forward	Interest in the person
Leaning back from a person	Lack of interest in the person, or rather shy or reserved
Back straight with chest out: "puffing up"	Aggression and/or high status

Open and closed posture

The table above shows the meaning of various body postures. In general, we can describe postures as "open" or "closed":

Open and closed body postures

- An open posture is one in which we can see the body (the torso), with arms and legs uncrossed and shoulders back. This can convey one of several messages: self-confidence, a relaxed non-defensive state or even an aggressive one.

- A closed position is one that closes up the body by a more stooped posture with arms across the body, or arms folded and legs crossed if sitting down. It is a very defensive posture and shows a lack of self-confidence or nervousness.

Postural echo

This refers to the tendency of two people, when sitting together, to adopt postures that are the mirror-image of each other. For example, one person may cross their legs from right to left whilst the other crosses them left to right. As one leans forward, so does the other. They may even synchronise hand positions and hair grooming. It tends to demonstrate that the two people are getting along well and are "on the same wavelength".

Two friends exhibiting postural echo

Gestures

Some everyday gestures and their meaning	
Beckoning finger	Come here
Shaking of fist	I'm very angry
Wave of arm	Goodbye
Wave of both arms	Pay attention to me/ I'm over here
Shake of head	No
Nod of head	I agree
Pointing of finger	Look at that

Culture and gestures

Some gestures are universal (the same in every culture). Saitz et al. (1972) found that pointing, shrugging, nodding of the head, clapping, beckoning, waving and thumbs down were common in more than one culture. These gestures may have evolved to serve a certain function; for example, Darwin suggested that head shaking (meaning "no") may have evolved from babies at the breast shaking their heads away when they have had enough.

However, the meaning of some gestures varies from culture to culture and can be a source of confusion or embarrassment. Gregor (1993) reports the case of a newly employed Asian engineer in an American company. As he was leaving his office for his first meeting, his secretary crossed her fingers in a gesture intended by her to wish him good luck. Unfortunately it rather confused and embarrassed him because in his country crossing your fingers is a sexual proposition.

Touch

- Touch is the most primitive form of social communication, as indicated by the fact that it is used by many species of animal and by very young children.
- The unwritten "rules" about touching vary between cultures and can be a major source of embarrassment and awkwardness. Touch can cause offence if used inappropriately.
- For example, in France men kiss each other, but this is considered inappropriate in Britain. When male politicians from Britain and France meet each other there is sometimes obvious discomfort from the British when being embraced by their French counterpart, however hard they try to hide it.
- Willis et al. (1994) found that in all cultures it is more accepted for females to touch other females than for men to touch other men, but there were large differences between cultures in their tolerance for same-sex touching. Spain was one of the most tolerant and Malaysia one of the least.
- Touch is an important part of many ceremonies (such as weddings, christenings and funerals).

Functions of touch

Jones et al. (1985) analysed 1500 touches and found 18 types of touch that could be grouped as follows:

Function of touch	Example
Positive affect	• Kissing • Stroking during sex
Playful	• Tickling • Rough and tumble
Control	• Hitting • Firm hold on the arm • Restraint
Ritual	• Bowing • Touching cap • Hand shaking

Mixed: e.g. greeting and affection	• Hug • Kiss
Task related	• A nurse/doctor touching a patient
Persuasion [Used deliberately or subconsciously to persuade others to do something for them. When asking a favour, people are far more likely to agree to it if you touch them while asking than if you don't. See study by Kleinke on p. 110 of *Psychology for GCSE Level, 2nd Edition*, for an example of how touch influences people]	• A light touch on the arm

Comparing verbal and non-verbal communication signals

STUDY: ARGYLE, ALKEMA AND GILMORE (1971)

Aim: To compare verbal and non-verbal signals as a way of judging someone on a friendly–hostile dimension.

Method: Three different verbal messages were devised that were considered friendly, neutral or hostile. They were then each read out using three different non-verbal styles: friendly, neutral or hostile. Therefore there were nine conditions in all, for example:

• A friendly message read in a friendly style.
• A friendly message read in a neutral style.
• A friendly message read in an unfriendly style.

Listeners were then asked to rate the people reading the messages on a scale of 1–7 as friendly or hostile.

Results: The non-verbal cues had five times the effect that the verbal ones had on the final rating. In other words, when a friendly message was read in a hostile tone, it was interpreted as hostile and unfriendly, and vice versa.

Conclusion: Non-verbal cues have far more effect than verbal cues. When the messages were in conflict, the verbal content (the actual message) was virtually ignored.

EVALUATION

➕ *Support from other studies*: These findings have been supported by studies using more realistic materials that have been taken from soap operas (Trimboli, 1984).

➖ *Findings may only be valid for simple messages*: This study only investigated a very straightforward message. It is not necessarily true that non-verbal cues would override the meaning of what was said in other messages. When studies have been done in which attitudes are expressed, the verbal content (i.e. what was actually said) was used to judge the speaker (Friedman, 1978).

Personal space

Definition

Personal space can be defined as a "portable, invisible boundary surrounding us, into which others may not trespass. It regulates how closely we interact with others, moves with us, and expands and contracts according to the situation in which we find ourselves" (Bell et al., 1996). In other words, our personal space is like an invisible bubble surrounding us into which people cannot move without causing us discomfort. It is a form of non-verbal communication because when we move away or towards someone (quite subconsciously) we are sending a message such as "that's quite close enough thank you" or "I like you, I want to be friends with you".

Personal space is roughly circular but with rather more space in front than behind. The size changes depending on the situation in which we find ourselves.

Cultural norms and personal space

Personal space is very much affected by culture. Different cultures have very different norms for how close they stand to others and how much they touch each other. Little (1968) examined cultural differences over 19 different social situations in a sample of Americans, Swedes, Greeks, Italians and Scots. They had to place dolls at distances that reflected where they would stand in real social situations, such as two good friends talking or a shop owner discussing the weather with his assistant. The findings showed considerable differences between cultures, as follows:

- The Greeks stood closest, the Americans next closest and the Scots the furthest away.
- There were considerable male–female differences between Greeks and Scots: with the Greeks it was the women who stood closer than the men but with the Scots the women stood further away than did the men.
- On average across all nations there was only a small gender difference, with the men standing slightly closer than the women.

Different cultures have different norms for personal space

Contact and non-contact cultures

Hall (1966) distinguished between "contact" and "non-contact" cultures.

Contact cultures	Non-contact cultures
(e.g. Mediterranean countries such as Italy and Spain, Latin American countries and many countries in the Middle East)	*(e.g. Britain, other northern European countries and the USA)*
Lots of physical contact between people	Limited physical contact
People enjoy the company of others	People keep themselves to themselves
Lots of social mixing	Not a great deal of informal socialising
View people from non-contact cultures as standoffish and snobbish, and feel offended by the distance they keep	View people from contact countries as invasive, intrusive, overfamiliar and are embarrassed and uncomfortable with them

Sex differences in personal space

Fisher and Byrne (1975) conducted a study in a university library in which confederates selected someone who was sitting on a table on their own and they either sat opposite them, one seat away or next to them. The researchers then asked the participant to complete a questionnaire about the experience, which asked questions about how the participant felt during the invasion of their personal space (e.g., how happy they felt, how attracted they were to the confederate, their perceived level of crowding, etc.). They found that males disliked being invaded by someone approaching from opposite them, but did not mind someone invading the space next to them. For females, the opposite results arose – they did not mind people invading the space opposite to them, but disliked invasion when someone sat next to them.

The researchers also observed where males and females placed their personal belongings and found sex differences – males were more likely to place their personal belongings in front of them, whilst females were more likely to place personal belongings next to them. This demonstrated that both males and females were placing barriers to defend against people invading from their least preferred direction.

To sum up:

- Males do not like to have their space invaded from the front.
- Females do not like to have their space invaded from the side.
- Both genders defend this invasion by placing barriers to stop people getting too close.

Individual differences in personal space

Personality influences personal space in the following ways:

- Extroverts (outgoing people) stand closer to others than do people with a quieter, inward temperament (although not all research supports this).
- Confident, assertive and self-assured people also stand closer than average.
- Anxious people tend to keep a greater distance between themselves and others, and this applies even more clearly to mentally ill people.
- Disruptive and aggressive teenagers also have large personal space.
- The stage of the menstrual cycle also appears to have some effect on personal space. Sanders (1978) found that women aged 17–27 years tended to have a larger personal space during the menstrual period compared to the middle of the cycle.

■ **Despite the above, personality on its own is difficult to relate to personal space. Generally, we need to take into account both the personality and other factors. For example, we need to consider the relationship between the people and the situation (is it a friendly encounter, an interview, an argument?).**

Status and personal space

Status affects personal space in the following ways:

- People of unequal status (boss and employee; teacher and pupil) tend to stand further apart than do equals.
- The person of higher status tends to face the other person, put their shoulders back, pull their body up to maximum height, fix their gaze on the eyes of the other person: all ways of emphasising their higher status.

- Lower status people tend to gaze at higher status people far more than the other way around, perhaps because the lower status person needs to know what is expected of them by the higher status person.
- Higher status people can usually outstare the lower status ones. This may be used to establish a "pecking order" in terms of gaze.

Contemporary practical implications of studies of non-verbal communication

Lie detection

Non-verbal communication may give clues to when people are lying, since they tend to have fidgety hands and feet, a high pitched tone or a quiver in the voice.

Obviously the ability to detect lying is quite important for the criminal justice system. In order to investigate whether people could be trained to detect lying, Ekman et al. (1991) compared four groups of professionals: police detectives, agents from US customs, people working for the CIA (Central Intelligence Agency) and people working for the Secret Service. The four groups were asked to watch a videotape and judge who was lying. The Secret Service agents were better than all of the other three, who were in fact no better at lie detection than ordinary members of the public.

Research indicates something strange – that the less information people receive, the better they are at detecting lies. For example, people can detect deception better if they only see the body of someone (on a videotape) than if they see the face as well. This is because people find it easier to lie with their face than with their body. With only the body to go by, the detection of a lie becomes easier. This has useful practical applications because it may give clues to whether a person is telling the truth when interviewed by the police. Nevertheless, clues from non-verbal communication need to be used carefully because any conclusions drawn from it are bound to depend to a certain extent on the interpretation of the observer. If you consider a suspect being interviewed, it is possible that they may be fidgety because they are nervous rather than because they are telling lies; in addition, some people are naturally more fidgety than others and if we have no previous knowledge of that individual it is difficult to interpret their behaviour.

OVER TO YOU

Now try the following revision activities:

1. Draw a table of two columns, one headed "contact cultures" and the other headed "non-contact cultures". Fill in the table by giving three

characteristics of each type of culture, arranged so they are describing differences between them (e.g. lots of social mixing/very little informal socialising).

2. Test yourself on the Sackeim et al. (1978) and the Argyle et al. (1971) studies by writing the headings "Aim", "Method", "Results", "Conclusion" and filling in the details. Go back and compare it with your textbook.

3. Write the following words/phrases on one side of separate pieces of card and the definition on the other:
   - Posture
   - Open posture
   - Closed posture
   - Postural echo

Then use the cards to test yourself on the meaning of these terms.

EXAMPLE EXAM QUESTIONS

1 George and Bill are having a conversation that is very polite and appears quite friendly if it is only judged on what is said. However, their body language indicates that they are quite hostile to one another.

(a) What is meant by *non-verbal communication*? **1 MARK**

(b) Give examples of **two** types of non-verbal communication shown by George or Bill that might indicate that they are not friendly but in fact are quite hostile to each other. **4 MARKS**

2 (a) Describe **one** study of non-verbal communication that looks at the relationship between facial expressions and the hemispheres of the brain (e.g. Sackeim, 1978). Include in your answer the reason why the study was conducted, the method used, the results obtained and the conclusion drawn. **4 MARKS**

(b) Evaluate this study. **3 MARKS**

3 (a) What is meant by *personal space*? **2 MARKS**

(b) What has research told us about the differences in how males and females use personal space? **4 MARKS**

MODEL ANSWER TO QUESTION 1

(a) Non-verbal communication is any way of conveying a message that does not involve words (or vocal sounds).

(b) One example could be the posture of George and Bill; they could be standing with a rigid posture and leaning away from each other with their chests puffed out. Another example is eye contact; they could be making very little eye contact with only occasional glances at each other.

DEVELOPMENT OF PERSONALITY

4

What's it about?

Our personality is obviously a crucial part of who we are; indeed some people would argue that a person's personality defines them as an individual. It follows, therefore, that a very important area of study for psychology concerns the definition and development of personality. What dimensions of personality are there? Why are people so different? Are they born with a particular set of personality traits or are these a product of their upbringing and life experiences? We are yet again considering the nature–nurture debate, this time as applied to what makes us who we are.

WHAT'S IN THIS UNIT?

The specification lists the following things that you will need to be able to do for the examination:

- Define personality, including temperament
- Describe and evaluate studies of temperament, including
  - Thomas (1977)
  - Buss and Plomin (1984)
  - Kagan (1991)
- Describe Eysenck's (1952) type theory of personality: extraversion, introversion, neuroticism
  - Describe personality scales, including the EPI and EPQ
- Evaluate Eysenck's type theory
- With respect to antisocial personality disorder (APD)
  - Outline the characteristics of APD
  - Describe and evaluate causes of APD
  - Biological: including the work of Raine (2000)
  - Situational: including the work of Farrington (1995) and Elander (2000)
- Describe and evaluate studies of the causes of APD
- Consider implications of research into APD

Key terms

Here is a list of important terms that you should learn in your revision. Try to write definitions for these after reading the chapter, and check your answers in the glossary on pp. 131–136. Essential terms that you *must* know in order to properly understand the topic are marked with an asterisk.

Antisocial personality disorder*	Introversion	Psychoticism
DSM-IV	Longitudinal study	Temperament*
Extraversion	Neuroticism	
	Personality*	

Definition of personality and temperament

- **Personality** refers to a relatively stable set of behaviours, thoughts and feelings that a person shows to others.
- **Temperament** refers to your *natural* disposition in terms of personality traits. That is, it refers to the personality you are apparently born with.

Description and evaluation of studies into temperament

STUDY: THOMAS ET AL. (1977 AND 1986)

This is the same longitudinal study with results published several times.

Aim: To investigate whether people respond to the environment in a similar way throughout life.

Method: A total of 85 New York families with around 136 children took part in a longitudinal study that had been running for 12 years. During the study, the researchers collected data about each child and their behaviour from parent interviews, school observations and teacher interviews.

Results: Three distinct groups emerged:

- Children labelled "easy" tended to be happier, adapted to situations much faster and were regular in their behaviour compared to the other two groups.

- Children labelled "difficult" tended to be much more demanding in their behaviour, were less flexible with their behaviours and tended to cry more.
- Children labelled "slow to warm up" initially did not react well to changes in their environment or to new environments.

Conclusion: As these characteristics remained stable over time, Thomas concluded that we are born with a temperament (i.e. it is innate).

EVALUATION

➕ There were several measures of the temperament, so reliability could be tested.

➕ It was a longitudinal study, so it did not rely on retrospective data collection.

➖ The measures may not be entirely accurate. There may be some subjectivity in the measurements.

➖ Just because the temperament is consistent over time, this does not mean it is innate. Being brought up in a stable environment might explain this.

STUDY: BUSS AND PLOMIN (1984)

Aim: To examine similarities in twins' temperament.

Method: A total of 228 identical twin pairs and 172 non-identical twin pairs were participants. They had three measures of personality:

- Emotional
- Active
- Sociable

Results: The correlations between the identical twins were positive and much higher than those for non-identical twins.

Conclusion: Temperament is largely genetic, as the identical twins were very similar on all measures of personality.

EVALUATION

➕ There was a large sample of twins, meaning that the results are likely to be generalisable.

➖ The research method was correlational, which means we cannot say that there is cause and effect, only that there is a relationship.

STUDY: KAGAN ET AL. (1991)

Aim: To test the idea that temperament is linked to allergies.

Method: A total of 528 relatives of 89 children formed the sample. The children were split between being either uninhibited (e.g. sociable, $n = 41$) or inhibited (e.g. shy, $n = 48$). These children had been tested at 21 months, 31 months and 7.5 years of age.

The relatives took part in a telephone interview asking them about a series of 63 medical symptoms alongside at least five psychological symptoms. It was recorded for each symptom if the answer was "yes" or "no".

Results: For the vast majority of symptoms there were no differences between the groups. However, for five symptoms there were statistically significant differences:

- Hayfever
- Eczema
- Stomach cramps
- Menstrual problems
- High social anxiety

More relatives of inhibited children reported the five symptoms.

Conclusion: It would appear that the same chemicals in our body that control hayfever symptoms also affect emotional mood. This could well be genetic; hence temperament is linked to these symptoms.

EVALUATION

➕ There was a large sample size, which makes it easier to generalise the results.

➕ The information about each child came from a number of sources, so it is likely that it is reliable.

➖ There was no information from doctors, which could have been used to assess the validity of the claims of the participants.

➖ They were forced into a yes/no choice. Is one episode of stomach cramps a "yes" or a "no"? There was not a "sometimes" choice!

Eysenck's type theory

Eysenck created two questionnaires, the Eysenck Personality Inventory (EPI) and Eysenck Personality Questionnaire (EPQ), to measure the personality types of people using yes/no questions. Once completed, a score can be given to show the level of Eysenck's personality factors, which are:

Extraversion (E score)	People scoring high on this scale tend to be more sociable and impulsive compared to low scorers (labelled introverts), who tend to be more cautious and not as social
Neuroticism (N score)	People scoring high on this scale tend to be more anxious, depressed and tense compared to low scorers, who tend to be more relaxed
Psychoticism (P score)	People who score high on this scale tend to be more aggressive, egocentric and cold compared to low scorers, who tend to be warm, more aware of others and not aggressive

- Eysenck was a firm believer in personality being genetic (he claimed up to two-thirds could be).
- He also believed that some of the personality traits were physiological.
- Introverts have higher levels of brain activity compared to extraverts. Therefore extraverts' brains are *stimulus hungry*, as their brains need to be stimulated more than introverts'!

Personality scales

Eysenck created two difference questionnaires to test out his ideas about personality:

- The Eysenck Personality Inventory (1965).
- The Eysenck Personality Questionnaire (1975).

The Eysenck Personality Inventory asks questions that measure extraversion and neuroticism.

Examples of the types of questions asked in Eysenck's Personality Inventory		
Are you fairly talkative when you are with a group of people?	YES ☐	NO ☐
When the odds are against you, do you still feel it is worth taking a chance?	YES ☐	NO ☐
Do you rely on friends to cheer you up?	YES ☐	NO ☐

The Eysenck Personality Questionnaire was developed to add the third dimension: psychoticism. Therefore participants completing this questionnaire can be scored for extraversion, neuroticism and psychoticism.

The traits associated with the three temperaments in Eysenck's model of personality		
Psychoticism	Extraversion	Neuroticism
Aggressive	Sociable	Anxious
Unsympathetic	Lack of reflection	Low self-esteem
Achievement-oriented	Impulsive	Moody

EVALUATION OF EYSENCK'S TYPE THEORY

● There are a number of competing theories of personality, for example, Rogers and Maslow. People have to self-actualise (reach their full potential) and decide on their own destiny and personality via free will. Therefore, it is incorrect to categorise people via E, N and P.

● *The Five-Factor Model* based on the work of Norman (1963) is another competing type theory. It states that there are obviously five main personality factors: extraversion, agreeableness (e.g. being cooperative), conscientiousness (e.g. being responsible), emotional stability (e.g. being calm in situations) and culture (e.g. being imaginative).

● Fahrenberg (1992) concluded that over many decades there had been a great deal of research into the link between physiology and personality, but none had really shown any.

● There is some support of a genetic element to personality. Neuroticism has been shown to be 80% inherited (Eysenck & Prell, 1951) and extraversion has been shown to be 62% inherited (Eysenck, 1956). Zuckerman (1989) reviewed four studies and concluded that both extraversion and neuroticism were 40–50% inherited.

Antisocial personality disorder (APD)

Definition and characteristics

Antisocial personality disorder (APD) involves a disregard for the rights of others that has been going on since the person was 15 years of age or younger. Only people over the age of 18 can be diagnosed with this disorder.

The DSM-IV states that a person with APD must have or show signs of the following symptoms:

1. Taking no notice of rules and breaking the law.
2. Telling lies and being deceitful.
3. Acting on impulse rather than planning ahead.
4. Being aggressive.
5. Being irresponsible.
6. Not being in the least sorry if they hurt other people.

One of the key factors that might account for the symptoms above is that people with APD may have a *lack of emotion*, both positive and negative – they don't feel happy, sad, disappointed, loving, angry, sympathetic, scared.

Causes of APD

Biological causes

Brain dysfunction

APD may be caused by malfunction of part of the brain, particularly two areas:

1. The amygdala, which is responsible for learning through negative consequences of our actions.
2. The prefrontal cortex, which enables people to learn social and moral behaviour.

STUDY: RAINE (2000)

Aim: To see if abnormalities in the prefrontal cortex are associated with APD.

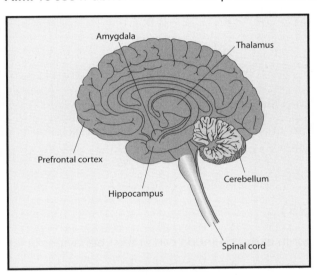

Method: 21 men diagnosed with APD and who had a history of serious violent crimes underwent an MRI scan. They were compared with 34 men with no history of violence.

Results: The APD group had an 11–14% reduction in the nerve cells of the pre-frontal cortex compared to normal males.

Conclusion: APD may be caused by deficits in the prefrontal cortex, the area of the brain responsible for a child's ability to learn to feel remorse and develop a conscience.

EVALUATION

➕ *An objective measure has been used*: This study uses brain scanning, which is fairly objective and therefore provides convincing evidence for the biological basis of APD.

➕ *Some important controls were used*: The study controlled for substance abuse and mental health problems, both of which could have been associated with the brain deficit.

➕ *The study has important applications*: Raine believes that biology is not destiny but early intervention is required for those with these brain deficits.

➖ *The study only used males*: Therefore it cannot be generalised to females.

➖ *Unrepresentative sample*: The men examined were all volunteers and so may not be typical of other APD sufferers.

Genetics

Several studies show that the fathers of people with APD tend to show antisocial behaviour. Ge et al. (1996) found that adopted children who have a biological parent with APD are more likely, as adults, to have APD than other adults.

Situational factors

The role of the family

- *Maternal deprivation/severe neglect*: Bowlby's theory of attachment (see p. 39 of *Psychology for GCSE Level, 2nd Edition*) provides an explanation for an affectionless personality that could result in APD. Also, McCord and McCord (1964) concluded that people who had been severely neglected by their parents could develop APD.
- *Inconsistent discipline*: A strict father and a lenient mother who gives in to the child's demands can encourage irresponsibility.

EVALUATION

➕ *Support from research*: Bowlby; McCord and McCord.

➖ *Other factors involved*: Many children brought up by parents whose discipline is poor never show signs of antisocial behaviour or a lack of concern for other people, so there are probably other factors involved.

STUDY: FARRINGTON (1995)

Aim: To investigate whether behaviour in early childhood can predict behaviour in later life.

Method: 411 males were followed up from age 8 to age 32. The characteristics investigated included:

- IQ (intelligence quotient) and school attainment.
- Antisocial behaviour.
- How parents treated their children.

Results: The main characteristics that predicted whether the child grew up to be an adult with APD were:

- Antisocial behaviour.
- Low IQ and school attainment.
- Poor child-rearing by the parents.
- The family is involved in crime.
- Impulsive behaviour.

Conclusion: In order to reduce the rates of APD in adults, it is necessary to tackle childhood problem behaviour.

STUDY: ELANDER ET AL. (2000)

Aim: To investigate childhood risk factors for APD.

Method: 225 pairs of twins who had been diagnosed with childhood disorders were investigated 10–25 years after diagnosis.

Results: Criminal behaviour and APD could be predicted from childhood disorders, mainly hyperactivity, conduct disorders and low IQ.

Conclusion: APD can be predicted from certain childhood disorders. This has implications for preventing the development of APD.

Implications of research into APD

- Elander et al. (2000) concluded that criminality could have been predicted from antisocial behaviour and/or major mental illness revealed earlier in life.
- Hagell (2003) points out that it is important to spot the factors in a child's early life that are associated with later APD. These factors include children who are difficult to manage from a very early age, who are in an abusive family and who have very few opportunities to feel worthwhile. In this way prevention may be possible.
- If children and families with a lot of risk factors are identified and helped when the children are quite young, then it is possible that the rates of APD in later life could be reduced. However, it is important to identify these children at a young age. Raine (2000) argues that it may be too late once they are old enough to be diagnosed with APD.

OVER TO YOU

Now try the following revision activities:

1. Using the research methods section of this book, list advantages and disadvantages of using a questionnaire/self-report style of personality test such as the EPI or EPQ.
2. On one side of a set of cards, write the names of the following studies (one per card). On the back of each card, write a one-sentence conclusion and test yourself. This will help you choose an appropriate study if given a choice in the exam.
   - Thomas (1977)
   - Buss and Plomin (1984)
   - Kagan (1991)

- **Raine (2000)**
- **Farrington (1995)**
3. **Draw a spider diagram with APD in the centre and the legs covering symptoms, biological explanations and situational explanations, presenting the sets of explanations in such a way as to provide a quick revision aid.**

EXAMPLE EXAM QUESTIONS

1 Outline what is meant by the term *personality*.   **2 MARKS**

2 (a) Briefly describe Eysenck's type theory of personality.   **4 MARKS**

(b) Evaluate Eysenck's type theory of personality.   **4 MARKS**

3 Below is a list of characteristics. Tick the **two** that describe antisocial personality disorder according to DSM-IV.   **2 MARKS**

(a) Happy-go-lucky attitude

(b) Dependency

(c) Deceitfulness

(d) Lack of intelligence

(e) Disregard for your own safety

(f) Surliness

4 Describe and evaluate the study by Raine (2000). Include in your answer the method used in the study, the results obtained, the conclusion drawn and an evaluation of the study. [*Use continuous prose.*]   **6 MARKS**

MODEL ANSWER TO QUESTION 4

Raine (2000) conducted an MRI scan of 21 men who had been diagnosed with APD and had committed violent crimes. They were compared with 34 healthy men with no such history of violence. It was found that there were about 11% fewer nerve cells in the prefrontal cortex of the APD sufferers than in the healthy controls. Raine concluded that APD could be caused by deficiencies in the part of the brain responsible for the development of moral standards. On the positive side, the study controlled for other factors that could be connected with brain deficits, such as drug abuse and mental health problems. It provides convincing evidence of a biological basis for APD. However, as all the participants were volunteer males, the results cannot necessarily be applied to women or to people who would not willingly volunteer to take part in such a study.

STEREOTYPING, PREJUDICE AND DISCRIMINATION

5

What's it about?

We live in a society that consists of many different social groups – men, women, Jews, Muslims, Catholics, southerners, northerners, teenagers – to name only a few. As we grow up, we develop attitudes towards some of these groups, often with very little if any knowledge of what they are really like. Sometimes these attitudes are prejudiced. In this chapter we will consider how these attitudes develop, what the difference is between stereotyping and prejudice and what discrimination involves. We will also consider and evaluate a very important social issue – that of attempting to reduce prejudice.

WHAT'S IN THIS UNIT?

The specification lists the following things that you will need to be able to do for the examination:

- Define stereotyping, prejudice and discrimination
- Stereotyping as oversimplification, leading to positive and negative evaluations
- Describe and evaluate studies of prejudice and of discrimination, including the work of:
  - ☐ Adorno (authoritarian personality)
  - ☐ Tajfel (in-groups and out-groups)
  - ☐ Sherif (Robbers' Cave)
- Explain prejudice and discrimination
- Describe ways of reducing prejudice and discrimination
- Evaluate ways of reducing prejudice and discrimination
- Describe contemporary implications of research into stereotyping, prejudice and discrimination, and their benefits and drawbacks

Key terms

Here is a list of important terms that you should learn in your revision. Try to write definitions for these after reading the chapter, and check your answers in the glossary on pp. 131–136. Essential terms that you *must* know in order to properly understand the topic are marked with an asterisk.

Authoritarian personality*	In-group*	Stereotyping*
Discrimination*	Out-group*	
F-Scale	Prejudice*	

Some important definitions

Stereotyping

Stereotyping involves holding beliefs about the characteristics of groups of individuals and assuming that each individual member of that group has those characteristics. Common stereotypes are those based on race, religion, social class, sex, sexuality and attractiveness.

Stereotypes are sometimes negative or positive and thus can form the basis of prejudiced attitudes and discrimination.

Not everyone conforms to stereotypes

Prejudice

Prejudice can be defined as "an attitude that predisposes us to think, feel, perceive and act in favourable or unfavourable ways towards a group or its individual members". Prejudice can be positive or negative, although it is usually associated with negative feelings.

Discrimination

Discrimination (social) involves the unequal treatment of individuals or groups based on arbitrary characteristics such as race, sex, ethnicity and cultural background.

The three components of a prejudiced attitude: ABC

Prejudice, like all attitudes, has three parts or components, which we can refer to as ABC.

Component of prejudice	Example
Affective – FEELINGS	"I hate people with tattoos"
Behavioural – ACTION	"I avoid people with tattoos"
Cognitive – BELIEFS	"People with tattoos are extremely aggressive"

Now we'll consider how these components apply to prejudiced attitudes.

Types of prejudice

There are many types of prejudiced attitudes. Four important ones are the following:

Sexism	A prejudice towards people based on their sex. It often (but not always) refers to contempt shown by men for women and may include discrimination against women
Ethnocentrism	The belief that one's own ethnic group, nation or religion is superior to all others
Racism	A prejudice towards people based on their race or ethnic group. It may involve hatred, rivalry or bad feeling between races. It is often related to ethnocentrism because it often includes the attitude that one's own racial group is superior to all others
Ageism	A prejudice based on age. It usually involves discrimination against the elderly

Studies of prejudice and discrimination

STUDY: THE "ROBBERS' CAVE": SHERIF ET AL. (1961)

See pp. 58–59 of *Psychology for GCSE Level, 2nd Edition*.

Aim: To look at the effects of group competition on prejudice and to investigate ways of reducing prejudice by the use of common goals.

Method: 22 boys aged 11–12 years took part in the study. They were all white and came from stable lower-middle-class homes. The boys were there for 3 weeks and the study can be divided into stages, each corresponding to approximately a week each:

- *Week 1*: The boys were separated into two matched groups and kept apart. Towards the end of the first week the researchers arranged that the boys would begin to be aware of each other.
- *Week 2*: A series of competitions was organised between the groups, with valued prizes and a team trophy.
- *Week 3*: The researchers deliberately set up a few "emergencies" that could only be sorted out with cooperation between the two groups, so that they had the opportunity to work towards a common goal (known as a superordinate goal – one that can only be achieved if everyone cooperates).

Sherif's Robbers' Cave experiment: The two groups compete in a tug-of-war

Results:

- *Week 1*: The boys formed their own group identity and gave themselves team names. Once the boys became aware of the presence of the other group there was a definite division into **in-groups** and **out-groups**.
- *Week 2*: The team identity increased whilst the unpleasantness between the two groups quickly got worse. There were fights and name calling, especially when one group won.
- *Week 3*: The boys worked together cooperatively; by the end of the week, cross-group friendships had formed.

Conclusion: Inter-group competition can result in the formation of in-groups and out-groups with prejudiced attitudes and discrimination. The use of superordinate goals can reduce prejudice.

EVALUATION

➕ *High ecological validity*: This is a field study. Because it reflects everyday behaviour, this type of study has high ecological validity, which means that it tells us something about how people act in their ordinary lives.

➕ *Implications*: It demonstrates the conditions under which prejudice can occur and the conditions needed to reduce this prejudice. This may be of use in trying to break down prejudice and stop discrimination in ordinary lives and in real-life situations.

- *Small sample size*: The study only involved a small number of people, all of whom were similar in terms of age, sex and cultural and social background. It therefore does not necessarily tell us much about how other groups, such as adults, younger children, girls or people from other cultural and social backgrounds, would respond in such a situation.

- *Ethical problems*: The boys had never consented to take part in this study and they were placed in quite unpleasant conditions with a lot of hostility and bad feeling. It could also be argued that it is wrong to induce prejudice in people, especially in impressionable youngsters.

STUDY: TAJFEL ET AL. (1971)

See pp. 61–63 of *Psychology for GCSE Level, 2nd Edition*.

Aim: To investigate the effects of splitting people into in-groups and out-groups.

Method: The participants were boys aged 14–15 years from the same school who knew each other well. They were asked to do a task and on the basis of this were divided into "underestimators" or "overestimators". In this way, an "in-group" and an "out-group" were established.

They were then asked to give real money rewards to other boys with whom they had come to the study. This was done when they were alone and it was completely confidential. No boy could give rewards to himself, nor could he identify who he was giving the money to, but he did know whether they were a member of his own group or the other group.

Results: The boys consistently rewarded their own group members more than those of the other group, despite the fact that they personally did not gain from it. Even when the amount of money that could be gained was more if they had been more generous to the out-group, they still preferred to allocate points in such a way that there was the maximum difference between the two groups in favour of their own group.

Conclusions: Once people are split into groups, no matter how random or trivial the criterion on which the groups are formed, they tend to like their group more, to treat other groups less well and to behave competitively towards the other group even when no one benefits from it.

EVALUATION

➕ *Important implications*: The results of this study have very important implications for arrangements we make in society. For example, Tajfel pointed to the need to be very careful about putting children into arbitrary groups, such as in "houses" at school.

➕ *Large sample size*: This study used ordinary school boys in quite large numbers, so the findings can be generalised to other such groups.

➖ *Bias in sampling*: The study only used boys from one school. We cannot therefore assume that girls, or people from other social and cultural backgrounds, will act in the same way.

➖ *Demand characteristics*: The boys may have assumed that they should discriminate against the other group and so acted as they thought they should.

STUDY: THE RESEARCH OF ADORNO ET AL.

See pp. 64–66 of *Psychology for GCSE Level, 2nd Edition*.

Aim: To investigate the roots of prejudiced attitudes, particularly anti-Semitism (prejudice against Jews).

Method: The researchers developed a personality questionnaire known as the *F-scale* (F is short for potential for Fascism), which measured a personality characteristic known as authoritarianism. People who score highly on this scale are said to have an **authoritarian personality**. The F-scale questionnaire measures nine personality characteristics that are believed to make up an authoritarian personality, including:

- Conventionalism.
- Authoritarian submission.
- Superstition.
- Puritanical sexual attitudes.

After administering this, the researchers interviewed 40 high scorers and 40 low-scoring individuals.

Results: The questionnaires showed that people who are highly prejudiced are not simply prejudiced against one specific group of people but towards all minority groups. Someone who is anti-Semitic (anti-Jewish) is also liable to be racist, homophobic and sexist.

There were some important differences between the two groups, particularly in their upbringing and relationships with their parents. The parents of the highly prejudiced group:

- Tended to be over-strict and punished them very harshly, often using corporal punishment (hitting, smacking, caning and so on).
- Had unrealistically high expectations of their children.
- Were very concerned about what other people thought of their children and wanted them to be seen as successful.

These high scorers showed a lot of hidden resentment towards their parents.

EVALUATION

✚ *Representative sample*: Adorno et al. interviewed a large number of people from all walks of life, so had a representative sample of the target population.

✚ *Thorough methodology*: The researchers used a range of questionnaires (four different types), not just one. They also used interviews on high and low scorers and this provides a rich source of data from the people who were interviewed.

⊖ *Serious design problems with the questionnaires*: On many statements, if you agreed it meant you had an authoritarian personality. This may have resulted in an overestimation of how authoritarian people are.

⊖ *Social desirability bias*: People may not have told the truth if they thought the expression of prejudice was not acceptable to society's values or to the researchers.

Explanations of prejudice and discrimination

Realistic group conflict theory

Realistic group conflict theory states that prejudice is the direct result of competition for valued resources. Such a threat can be based on actual resources such as money, housing or power. It can also be symbolic, a threat to one's cultural ideals, values and customs. The group that has less in terms of land, jobs and power becomes frustrated and resentful, and the advantaged group feels threatened and on the defensive, so before long there is conflict.

EVALUATION

✚ *Support from research and everyday life*: Studies such as Robbers' Cave (Sherif et al. 1961) support this theory. There are also many instances in ordinary everyday life when prejudice appears to be rooted in groups competing for valued resources.

⊖ *It cannot account for all instances of prejudice*: Although conflict may account for how prejudice arises in certain situations, it cannot account for it all. Other theories have value.

Social identity theory (Tajfel, 1982)

Social identity theory states that prejudice results from people's motivation to boost their self-esteem through a positive social identity. People who have low self-esteem identify themselves with successful groups and increase their self-esteem by belittling, criticising and denigrating the out-groups. In this way they gain a positive social identity.

EVALUATION

✢ *Support from research*: Many studies, including those by Tajfel et al., have supported social identity theory. For example, Fein and Spencer (1993) showed that people of low self-esteem are especially likely to denigrate out-groups and that their self-esteem rises when they do so.

⊖ *It cannot account for cultural variations in prejudice*: Cultural variations in prejudice are probably the result of differences in social norms between cultures rather than due to issues of self-esteem.

⊖ *It cannot account for all instances of prejudice*: There are lots of other factors that may lead to prejudiced attitudes, such as upbringing (socialisation) and social norms (the attitudes that are acceptable within a community).

The authoritarian personality theory

The authoritarian personality theory states that prejudice is the result of a certain type of person-ality, known as an authoritarian personality, that predisposes people to have prejudiced attitudes.

The characteristics of an individual with an authoritarian personality can be summed up as:

- A rigid adherence to very traditional, conventional values.
- The belief in harsh punishment for violation of traditional norms.
- An extreme need to submit to those in higher authority, together with enormous admiration for "strong" leaders.
- A lot of hostility and anger in general, but particularly directed towards minority groups.

Such individuals have considerable resentment and hostility towards their parents that is *repressed* into the unconscious mind. This hatred is *displaced* onto minority groups. People who are authoritarian have no idea that they are really angry at their parents. They believe that they have a right to be angry at minority groups and to disapprove of anyone who disagrees with their point of view.

EVALUATION

➕ *Evidence from personality types and upbringing*: The personality pattern described by Adorno et al. (rigidity of thought, traditional attitudes, intolerance, aggression) is characteristic of highly prejudiced individuals. There is also a large body of evidence to indicate that people who are very rigid, conservative and prejudiced have been brought up in the way Adorno described, with a great deal of corporal punishment and little chance to express their own opinions.

➖ *Methodological problems with evidence*: The questionnaires used to support the theory were not well designed (see earlier study by Adomo et al.).

➖ *It cannot account for all instances of prejudice*: There are lots of other factors that may lead to prejudiced attitudes, such as social norms (the attitudes that are acceptable within a community).

Reducing prejudice

Establishing superordinate (common) goals

One way of reducing prejudice is for both in-groups and out-groups to work in a non-competitive way to achieve a superordinate goal. When groups work together to achieve common goals that benefit everyone, prejudice can sometimes be broken down and friendships established.

In Sherif's Robbers' Cave experiment, the superordinate goal of having to cooperate to fix a leaking pipe achieved harmony between the warring groups of boys, so that cross-group friendships formed

EVALUATION

➕ *Support from research*: Studies like Sherif's have shown that cooperation between people who are of equal status and trying to achieve a common goal does break down stereotypes, increase liking and reduce prejudice.

⊖ *It only works under certain circumstances*: This strategy will only work if the people involved are successful in completing the task. If they fail, they simply blame each other and this can make matters worse.

The jigsaw approach (Aronson et al., 1978)

This involves groups of children of different backgrounds working on a specially designed common task in such a way that they can all make a valuable contribution towards achieving the end goal. Each individual was given a specific task and had to research information and teach it to the rest of the group, so each child becomes an "expert" in turn.

EVALUATION

⊕ *Successful in improving self-esteem*: This means that it is also likely to reduce prejudice. It also increased a liking for school and improved academic performance.

⊕ *Uses young children*: This is good because positive attitudes towards other ethnic groups fostered in the young are liable to stay with them for a lifetime.

⊖ *It has limited application (use)*: Since it is only possible to use it on school children, it does not help in the reduction of prejudice in older people.

Demonstrating the effects of discrimination

Elliot (1968) divided a class of 7–8-year-olds into "blue eyes" and "brown eyes" and discriminated against one group on the basis of eye colour. On the first day of the study the blue-eyed children were superior but on the second day the brown-eyed children were superior. The superior group were given privileges and encouraged to look down on the inferior group and not to play with them. The children discriminated against the "out-group"; the situation was unhappy and divisive.

The purpose was to show children what it was like to be discriminated against, so that they did not do it in future. Elliot discussed with the children their experiences over the exercise and felt that they did have a greater understanding of discrimination.

EVALUATION

- *Long-lasting effects*: Some 30 years later the participants thought the experience had been really worthwhile. They reported being much more aware of prejudice and tried hard to be non-prejudiced themselves.

- *Can be applied to many groups*: It has been used with many people, mainly adults, to increase awareness of the effects of discrimination and therefore to reduce it.

- *Ethical problems*: It can cause a great deal of distress and antisocial behaviour. Jane Elliot herself advises that it should not be done unless the individual leading the group is extremely well trained.

Optimal contact between older and young people within a family context

Early investigators of prejudice reduction suggested that simply increasing the amount of contact between in-groups and out-groups might reduce prejudice between the two groups, but it soon became apparent that contact alone was not sufficient to change attitudes and that in some circumstances it may make it worse.

In the context of looking at increased contact between groups, Harwood et al. (2005) investigated the reduction of prejudice in young people towards older ones by looking at the relationship that students had with grandparents. They found that the most important factor that resulted in them not having negative ageist attitudes was the extent to which they had a positive relationship with a grandparent *and* saw them as representative of the older age group. So, one way of reducing prejudice is to have regular contact with grandparents who are seen as positive role models for elderly people.

EVALUATION

➕ This is important research because young children easily recognise different age categories and often have negative stereotypes about older people. Any research that helps to reduce this is useful.

➕ This research points to the importance of regular contact between grandparents and children.

➖ It is limited to helping with prejudice between young and much older people, so it does not apply to all prejudice. It will not, therefore, help to reduce prejudice such as racism.

➖ The information regarding contact between students and grandparents was gathered from interviews, which may not be reliable.

Contemporary practical implications of research into stereotyping, prejudice and discrimination: Using TV shows to reduce prejudice

Schiappa et al. (2005) believe that through the medium of television, viewers actually develop a relationship with characters and that this relationship (which he calls a *parasocial relationship*) leads to lessened prejudice. He has conducted experimental investigations into the effect of TV shows on prejudice reduction:

- 150 students watched 10 early episodes of "Six Feet Under", a programme sympathetic towards gays. Their level of prejudice towards gay men significantly reduced.
- 160 students were randomly assigned to one of two groups of 80 participants. The experimental group watched episodes of a programme called "Queer Eye for the Straight Guy", whereas the control group watched a stand-up comedy special. Those in the experimental group showed a significant reduction in prejudice compared to how they felt before watching the programmes, whereas the control group did not change.
- Schiappa et al. (2006) conducted a correlational study of the effects of TV on prejudice against gays and believe that the evidence indicates that watching programmes designed to reduce prejudice against gays is effective.

Schiappa points out that this research is of importance because it is virtually the only research that has shown that TV can have a positive influence on prejudice. Almost all other research has focused on how TV can increase prejudice.

OVER TO YOU

Now try the following revision activities:

1. Write the following words or phrases onto separate cards, with the definition on the back:
   - Stereotyping
   - Prejudice
   - Discrimination

   Now test yourself (or get a friend/family member to test you) by reading the word or phrase and then giving the definition.

2. Write the letters ABC down one side of a piece of paper. Now, using these initial letters, complete each word so that it gives the components of a prejudiced attitude. Give an example of how this component might be shown for:
   - Sexism
   - Racism
   - Homophobia
   - Ageism

3. Draw a storyboard to illustrate the three weeks of the Robbers' Cave study, with two pictures per week.

4. Draw a mind map to illustrate Adorno's work. Include the research, the limitations of the research, the characteristics of an authoritarian personality and the upbringing that might result in that personality.

EXAMPLE EXAM QUESTIONS

1 Read the following conversation between two students:

Mary: "When we do practical work, why does Mr Jones (the science teacher) always pay more attention to your group than ours?"

Tom: "Because we're boys and you're girls and he thinks boys are more interested in science than are girls."

Mary: "Well that's not fair, it's discrimination."

With reference to this conversation:

(a) Explain what is meant by the term *stereotyping*. **3 MARKS**

(b) Explain what is meant by the term *discrimination*. **4 MARKS**

2 Describe **one** study by Sherif on prejudice and discrimination. Include in your answer the reason why the study was conducted, the method used, the results obtained and the conclusion drawn. **4 MARKS**

3 Using your knowledge of psychology, describe and evaluate **one** way in which prejudice could be reduced. [*Use continuous prose.*] **6 MARKS**

MODEL ANSWER TO QUESTION 1

[*Note that it is important to learn these definitions for the exam but you MUST apply them to the particular example they give in order to get full marks.*]

(a) Stereotyping involves holding beliefs about the characteristics of groups of individuals and assuming that each individual member of that group has those characteristics. In the example, Mr Jones is accused of stereotyping the girls as not being interested in science just because they are girls.

(b) Discrimination involves the unequal treatment of people, so it means treating someone favourably or unfavourably. In the example, the boys are being treated favourably by Mr Jones because they are given more attention than the girls, who are therefore being treated unfavourably.

LEARNING

6

What's it about?

Psychologists from the learning/behavioural approach believe that all animals (including humans) learn through the same general laws of stimulus–response. In this chapter, we will look at these laws of learning and consider how different types of conditioning shape behaviour. Learning theories help to explain how animals learn to perform "tricks" and the reasons why humans behave in the way they do. We will also consider the learning theory approach to ways in which we can alter behaviour and thereby treat phobias and other problem behaviours.

WHAT'S IN THIS UNIT?

The specification lists the following things that you will need to be able to do for the examination:

■ Describe the principles of classical conditioning: unconditioned stimulus; unconditioned response; conditioned stimulus; conditioned response; extinction; spontaneous recovery; generalisation; discrimination; the contributions of Pavlov

■ Describe the principles of operant conditioning: Thorndike's Law of Effect and the contributions of Skinner; behaviour shaping; the distinction between positive reinforcement, negative reinforcement and punishment

■ Describe and evaluate attempts to apply conditioning procedures to the treatment of phobias (flooding and systematic desensitisation) and to change unwanted behaviour (aversion therapy and Token Economy), and the ethical implications of such attempts

Key terms

Here is a list of important terms that you should learn in your revision. Try to write definitions for these after reading the chapter, and check your answers in the glossary on pp. 131–136. Essential terms that you *must* know in order to properly understand the topic are marked with an asterisk.

Aversion therapy*	Law of Effect	Reciprocal inhibition
Conditioned response*	Negative punishment*	Secondary reinforcer
Conditioned stimulus*	Negative reinforcement*	Spontaneous recovery*
Discrimination*	Neutral stimulus*	Systematic desensitisation*
Extinction*	Positive punishment*	Token Economy*
Flooding*	Positive reinforcement*	Unconditioned response*
Generalisation*	Primary reinforcer	Unconditioned stimulus*

Classical conditioning

Classical conditioning is all about learning through association.

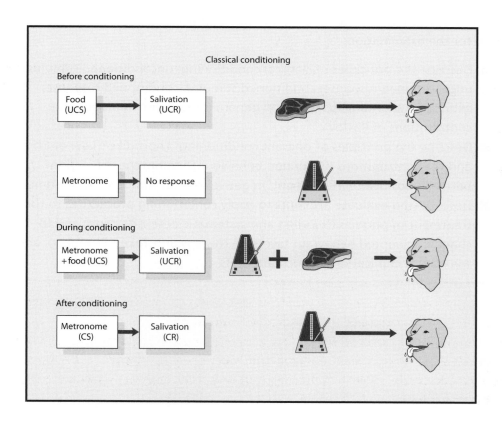

An example

Pavlov already knew that dogs salivate when they smell meat powder. Every time the powder was given to the dogs he sounded a metronome (a device that clicks at set intervals). He repeated this a few times. Then, he sounded the metronome *without* the meat powder and noticed that each dog still salivated.

Other important terms linked to classical conditioning

- **Generalisation**: This occurs when we produce a **conditioned response** to a stimulus that is *similar* but not the same as the **conditioned stimulus**.
- **Extinction**: This occurs when the conditioned stimulus no longer produces the conditioned response.
- **Spontaneous recovery**: This occurs after extinction. Suddenly, in the presence of the conditioned stimulus, the conditioned response reappears!
- **Discrimination**: This occurs when we produce a conditioned response to only *one* specific stimulus, even if there are similar ones in the environment.

Operant conditioning

Operant conditioning is all about learning through consequences. It is a form of conditioning using **reinforcements (rewards)** or **punishment**.

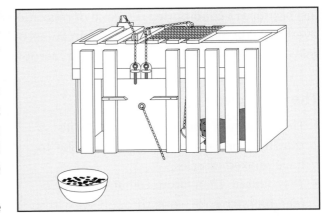

Edward Thorndike placed a hungry cat in a puzzle box, with food outside. The box was set up so that if the cat pulled on a piece of string inside the box, a catch would be released and the door (via a lever press mechanism) would open.

On the first trial, the cat took a long time to escape. The cat moved around the box and *by chance* tugged on the piece of string and released the catch on the door. Each time the cat was placed back in the box, it escaped more and more quickly.

From his study Thorndike created the *Law of Effect*, which states that if behaviour is followed by a pleasurable experience, the organism will be more likely to repeat that behaviour. However, if behaviour is followed by something that is not pleasurable, then the organism will be less likely to repeat that behaviour.

Burrhus F. Skinner took Thorndike's ideas to a wider audience by introducing a series of terms that are still used to explain how operant conditioning works. They are as follows:

	Positive	Negative
Reinforcement	The addition of something nice (e.g. reward) that increases the probability of that behaviour being repeated (pocket money for cleaning your room)	The removal of something aversive (not nice) that increases the probability of that behaviour being repeated (you no longer get shouted at if you clean your room)
Punishment	The addition of something aversive (not nice) that decreases the probability of that behaviour being repeated (being told off for stealing sweets)	The removal of something nice that decreases the probability of that behaviour being repeated (removal of TV or games console from bedroom for being naughty)

Behaviour therapy

Systematic desensitisation

Systematic desensitisation works on the idea that the phobia can be *unlearnt*. The end point should recondition the patient so that the conditioned stimulus (which will be the phobic stimulus) produces a conditioned response of relaxation rather than fear. For example, instead of being overly fearful of heights when flying in an aeroplane, a person is taught to think of a calm and relaxing environment when they sit in an aeroplane.

The principles

- The patient is taught relaxation skills so that they understand what it feels like to have relaxed muscles.
- The patient then produces an anxiety or fear hierarchy to work through with the therapist.
- You can only move up the hierarchy of fear once each stage has been successfully completed, which means when the patient is showing signs of relaxation at that stage in the hierarchy.

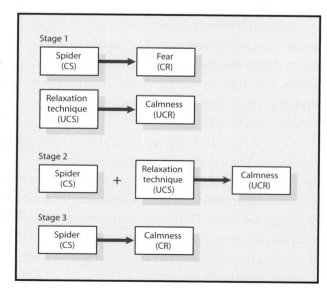

You can see from the diagram that in the conditioning phase there are competing responses of fear and relaxation. This is called *reciprocal inhibition*, which means that it is impossible to experience both emotions at the same time.

EVALUATION

➕ Capafons, Sosa and Avero (1998) reported that their 20 patients with a fear of flying who had several sessions working through their anxiety hierarchy became much less fearful of flying after the study ended.

➕ Zettle (2003) showed that systematic desensitisation can be applied to people who fear maths. Anxiety decreased markedly for those who completed their systematic desensitisation, even though their maths ability never changed!

➕ Ventis, Higbee and Murdock (2001) found that both relaxation techniques and simply laughing at the phobic stimulus were effective in reducing the fear in arachnophobics.

➖ There is a lack of follow-up studies to see if the patient is still cured of their phobia.

➖ Some psychologists believe that even though you move slowly up a hierarchy of fear, you are still being unethical by making people confront their phobias.

Flooding

The patient is exposed to the largest anxiety-provoking stimulus straight away (usually direct contact with the stimulus: this is called *in vivo*). Obviously, the patient is going to feel extreme levels of fear but this dies off quite rapidly as the body cannot sustain such a high level of arousal for a long time. The patient quickly learns that there is now nothing to be fearful of! The association between the phobic stimulus and fear has been broken, to form a new relationship of the phobic stimulus producing calm. An example might be sending someone sky diving because they have a fear of heights!

EVALUATION

➖ Many psychologists believe that this therapy is *unethical* because it causes distress, both physiologically and psychologically, to the patient.

➕ However, other psychologists would argue that the end outcome of curing the phobia is enough to justify the high distress caused in the short term.

➖ Even though this technique is used by psychologists, there have been hardly any studies testing its effectiveness.

Aversion therapy

- This follows the principle of associating a noxious stimulus (something horrid) with an already conditioned stimulus to produce a different conditioned response.
- After repeated "new" associations, the unwanted behaviour (conditioned stimulus) decreases, as it is now associated with something noxious.
- Aversion therapy has been used on alcoholics, to "cure" people of homosexuality or to treat sex offenders such as paedophiles.
- An example would be making a person take an emetic drug (it makes you vomit) every time they drink an alcoholic drink!

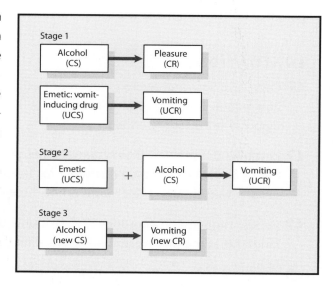

EVALUATION

- A great number of psychologists believe that aversion therapy for homosexuals is highly unethical. Who has the right to change someone else's behaviour just because they consider it to be "abnormal" or "atypical"?

- If the aversion therapy is combined with some social skills training, it has been shown repeatedly to be effective for paedophiles (Davison & Neale, 1998).

- Even though the behaviour that needs to be changed is not totally eliminated, it provides the patient with a greater control over that behaviour (Monaghy, 1994).

- Cautela (1966) reported that *covert sensitisation* as a form of aversion therapy is effective. The patient simply has to imagine unpleasant circumstances (e.g. a cocaine addict pictures himself just beginning to snort and then straight away visualises being violently ill).

The Token Economy

In an institution like a prison or school, a **Token Economy** can be set up.

- People are rewarded with tokens for appropriate behaviour that can be exchanged for privileges and other rewards.
- The tokens (called a secondary reinforcer) themselves are worthless but they can be exchanged for something that is needed, such as food (called a primary reinforcer) or access to activities they would not normally have.

- The institution sets a "price" on each primary reinforcer or activity so that each person has to earn them (e.g. in a prison, a prisoner may have to earn five tokens to watch some TV).
- People exchange their tokens at the rates set by the institution (in a similar way to when we buy products).
- The overall theme of the Token Economy is to promote good and appropriate behaviour with rewards, whilst ignoring bad or inappropriate behaviour.

EVALUATION

⊖ There is the ethical dilemma of deliberately changing a person's behaviour without consent. There could be problems of people in authority abusing the system and making prisoners, for instance, do more and more for one token – changing the boundaries unfairly just because they can.

⊕ In a classic early study, Ayllon and Azrin (1968) set up a Token Economy in a mental hospital. It was highly effective at controlling unwanted behaviour and encouraging wanted behaviour in a group of schizophrenics.

⊖ The outside world is not controlled and does not give out tokens for appropriate behaviour. Therefore, outside the hospital or prison the unwanted behaviour could quickly reappear as appropriate behaviour is no longer rewarded with tokens.

⊕ Other studies have shown that Token Economy procedures can be effective in increasing appropriate behaviour in emotionally disturbed youths (Hogan & Johnson, 1985), reducing impulsive behaviour in academically handicapped children (Errickson, Wyne & Routh 1973) and reducing swearing in institutionalised adolescents (Feindler & Elder, 1977).

OVER TO YOU

Now try the following revision activities:

1. Write the words *Unconditioned Stimulus, Unconditioned Response, Conditioned Stimulus, Conditioned Response* and *Neutral Stimulus* on separate index cards. On the reverse of each, write what they refer to in the Pavlov study. Then you can attempt to place them in the correct order, turn them over and see if you are correct (see p. 259 of *Psychology for GCSE Level, 2nd Edition*).
2. Again, write all of the key terms on separate index cards, with the definitions on the reverse. Get someone to hold up a card so that you can see either the term or the definition. You then have to identify what the term or definition is.

EXAMPLE EXAM QUESTIONS

1 What is the Law of Effect? **2 MARKS**

2 Describe what happens during classical conditioning. **5 MARKS**

3 What is punishment? **2 MARKS**

4 Describe and evaluate **one** technique to change unwanted behaviours in humans. In your answer you may wish to consider ethics. **8 MARKS**

MODEL ANSWER TO QUESTION 1

The Law of Effect was created by Thorndike after watching cats escape from a puzzle box. The law states that if a behaviour is followed by a pleasurable outcome, then we are more likely to do it again. However, if it is followed by a not-so-pleasurable outcome, then we are less likely to do it again.

7

SOCIAL INFLUENCE

What's it about?

Social psychology is about how we interact with other people when by ourselves or when in groups. These interactions help to shape who we are and how we act in subsequent similar and different situations. This helps us to perceive the world in a particular way. It also helps us to understand the world we live in. The area of focus for this broad topic in psychology is obedience – why are some people obedient and why are some people defiant? The factors that may stop people being obedient or change their obedience levels are also considered by social psychologists.

WHAT'S IN THIS UNIT?

The specification lists the following things that you will need to be able to do for the examination:

■ Define conformity, obedience, social loafing and deindividuation
■ Describe and evaluate studies into conformity, obedience, social loafing and deindividuation
■ Explain factors affecting conformity, obedience, social loafing and deindividuation
■ Explain factors affecting bystander intervention
■ Describe and evaluate studies into bystander intervention, including Latané and Darley (1968), Batson *et al.* (1983), Piliavin, Rodin and Piliavin (1969) and Schroeder *et al.* (1995)
■ Consider contemporary practical implications of studies and research into social influence and their benefits and drawbacks

Key terms

Here is a list of important terms that you should learn in your revision. Try to write definitions for these after reading the chapter, and check your answers in the glossary on pp. 131–136. Essential terms that you *must* know in order to properly understand the topic are marked with an asterisk.

Anonymous	Debriefing	Laboratory experiment
Authority figure	Defiance	Obedience*
Autokinetic effect	Deindividuation*	Participants
Bystander intervention	Ecological validity	Protection of
Collectivist	Extraneous variables	participants
Confederates	Individualistic	Right to withdraw
Conformity*	Informed consent	Social loafing*

Definitions of conformity, obedience, social loafing and deindividuation

- **Conformity** is when people behave in a certain way because of the pressure exerted on them by other group members.
- **Obedience** is when people behave in a certain way because they comply with the demands of an authority figure.
- **Social loafing** refers to situations when a person is likely to put in *less* effort in a group task. As a group is working towards some form of common goal, the individual members of that group put in less effort compared to what they would do if they were individually responsible for that task!
- **Deindividuation** refers to situations when a person, in a group, loses their sense of individuality or personal identity and personal responsibility for their actions. This is due to decreased awareness of one's actions when part of a large body of people. Therefore you just "go along with the crowd".

Description and evaluation of studies into conformity

STUDY: ASCH (1955)

See pp. 29–30 of *Psychology for GCSE Level, 2nd Edition*.

Aim: To see how the judgements of others in a group affect the decisions of an individual on a simple task.

Method: In the initial study, a group of seven to nine college students (all male) were assembled in a classroom. Not known to the participant, the other people were confederates (they were in on the experiment). In all, there were 123 participants. The experimenter held up two cards and asked the group which line on the right-hand card was the same length as line X. Each person answered in turn. The true participant answered last or next to last. On the first two trials the confederates stated the correct answer. However, on the third trial the confederates stated the wrong answer.

Results: In the trials where the confederates gave the wrong answer, the true participants also got it wrong (i.e. conformed) on 36.8% of them. However, 25% of participants *never* once conformed to a wrong answer that the confederates gave.

Conclusion: Most people will conform to the majority even on a very simple task.

EVALUATION

⊕ The research method used was a **laboratory experiment**. This means that Asch could confidently conclude that the set-up was directly affecting the conformity rates.

⊕ The task was not ambiguous. That is, there was a definite answer and the task was easy to measure. Compare this to the task used by Sherif below.

⊖ The study lacks **ecological validity**. That is, the task may not represent whether we would conform in a real-life situation.

⊖ Ethical issues: The participants were put under psychological stress and made to feel unfomfortable.

STUDY: SHERIF (1935)

See pp. 30–31 of *Psychology for GCSE Level, 2nd Edition*.

Aim: Sherif was interested in how people may change their individual view once placed in a group situation.

Method: Sherif tested conformity via an illusion called the **autokinetic effect** (see p. 31 of *Psychology for GCSE Level, 2nd Edition*). The effect is simple. Participants entered a darkened room where they could see a dot of light. They were asked to estimate how far it moved. Once the participants had given their estimations of movement (the light never moved) they were placed in groups. During their time in a group they were asked to discuss just how far the light moved. Sherif had, however, selected people who had reported a large movement, a medium movement and a small movement. After the discussion Sherif asked the participants to re-estimate how much the light had moved.

Results: Estimations did change after the discussion. A *group norm effect* tended to be seen. That is, people changed their estimations towards the average for the group.

Conclusion: People tend to conform more after discussion.

EVALUATION

✚ It was a laboratory experiment, so Sherif could be confident that the group discussion directly affected the final responses of the participants.

➖ The study lacks ecological validity. That is, the task may not represent whether we would conform in a real-life situation.

➖ The task itself was ambiguous. By this we mean that there was no real answer as the dot never moved. Participants were not being tested with something straightforward, as in the Asch study above.

Factors affecting conformity

See p. 31 of *Psychology for GCSE Level, 2nd Edition*.

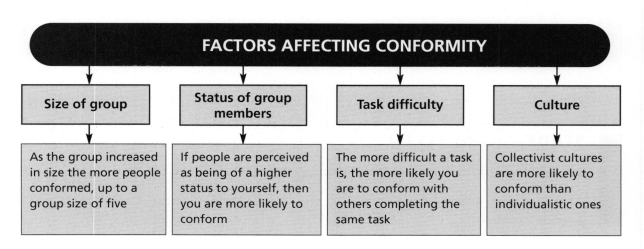

FACTORS AFFECTING CONFORMITY			
Size of group	**Status of group members**	**Task difficulty**	**Culture**
As the group increased in size the more people conformed, up to a group size of five	If people are perceived as being of a higher status to yourself, then you are more likely to conform	The more difficult a task is, the more likely you are to conform with others completing the same task	Collectivist cultures are more likely to conform than individualistic ones

Description and evaluation of studies into obedience

STUDY: MILGRAM (1963)

Aim: Milgram wanted to test out "destructive obedience" in a laboratory.

Method: Milgram advertised for participants (see newspaper announcement on p. 17 of *Psychology for GCSE Level, 2nd Edition*). Forty participants were then used in the study. Each participant met a Mr Wallace (a confederate) thinking that he was also a participant in the study. However, it was always "fixed" so that the participant was the teacher whilst Mr Wallace was the learner.

After this, Mr Wallace was seen being strapped into an "electric chair" device in the next room. The participant then left to sit in front of the "shock generator" in the next room. He was told that he would read out a series of word pairs (e.g. *blue box*). After reading out the pairs, he was instructed to read just one word (e.g. the word *blue* from the pair mentioned) followed by four words (three random ones and the real one – in this case, *pair*).

The participant was instructed that if Mr Wallace got one of them wrong they were to give him an electric shock via the "shock generator". The first button was for 15 volts and then every button after that increased the shock by 15 volts. The first incorrect answer would therefore get 15 volts, then 30 volts, then 45 volts and so on. This continued until the participant reached 450 volts! If the participant said that they did not want to continue, then the experimenter had to "prod" them verbally. When the participant had given Mr Wallace the 300-volt shock, Mr Wallace would hit the wall repeatedly so that the participant could hear it. After that point, Mr Wallace did not answer another word-pair task but participants were still instructed by the researcher to continue administering shocks.

Results: All of the participants gave a minimum of 300 volts to Mr Wallace and 65% gave 450 volts despite it having XXX above the button. Some continued to give 450 volts repeatedly, as Mr Wallace's silence meant a wrong answer.

Conclusion: The study clearly demonstrated that people do show high levels of obedience to an authority figure when they are allowed to punish someone for getting a task wrong.

EVALUATION

✪ It was a laboratory-based study, so Milgram could be confident that the situation the participants were placed in directly affected the shocks given by the participants.

✪ He did follow up the participants to make sure that they were all fine months after participating. Virtually all of the participants were pleased to have taken part in the experiment.

- Lacks ecological validity. That is, the task may not represent whether we would be obedient in a real-life situation.

- It is not ethical because Milgram did not get informed consent (nowhere on the advertisement does it state the true aim), was deceitful, did not allow participants the right to withdraw and placed all of them under high levels of psychological stress.

STUDY: HOFLING ET AL. (1966)

Aim: To see whether nurses were obedient to a potentially life-threatening order given to them by a doctor.

Method: A total of 22 nurses took part in the experiment. Each of the nurses was telephoned by a doctor (given a name that was not known to the nurse, e.g. Dr. Hanford in one case) and told to give a patient 20 milligrams (mg) of the drug "Astroten". The nurses were not aware that the pink pills inside the Astroten box were simply glucose tablets! On the box of Astroten it clearly stated that the usual dose was 5 mg and the maximum daily dose was 10 mg. Within 48 hours of the study, each of the nurses was interviewed and reassured that no harm had been done.

Results: Of the 22 nurses in the study, 21 simply completed the telephone call and gave the patient 20 mg of Astroten. The average length of telephone call was around 2 minutes. This indicates that the nurses offered no resistance and simply followed the orders of an authority figure.

Conclusion: Hofling had shown that people are obedient in real-life situations (and life-threatening situations!). It should be noted that a group of 21 student nurses were given the scenario on paper and asked what they would do. All 21 stated that they would never have given the patient Astroten.

EVALUATION

- The study has some level of ecological validity. That is, as the situation was "real" Hofling et al. could believe that their findings do relate to real-life nurse behaviour.

- There may have been many **extraneous variables**, which could have affected the nurses' responses (remember that in a laboratory you can control for these variables).

- Ethical issues: Many psychologists believe that Hofling et al. placed the nurses under psychological stress and did not get any **informed consent** from them.

Also see p. 22 of *Psychology for GCSE Level, 2nd Edition*, for the replication by Rank and Jacobson (1977).

Factors affecting obedience

See pp. 22–28 of *Psychology for GCSE Level, 2nd Edition*.

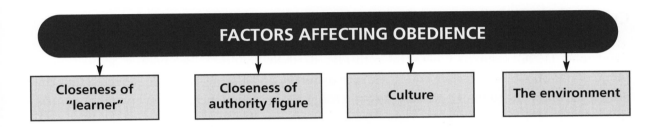

Closeness of "learner"

The three experiments that looked at the closeness of the learner were:

- *Voice feedback*. In this study Milgram got Mr Wallace to shout out the responses to the shocks.
- *Proximity*. In this study Milgram got Mr Wallace to be in the same room as the participant.
- *Touch-proximity*. In this study Milgram got Mr Wallace to place his hand onto a "shock plate".

Condition	Participants who gave 450 volts	Participants who gave 300 volts	Mean voltage given by the participants
Original	65.0%	100.0%	405 V
Voice feedback	62.5%	75.0%	360 V
Proximity	40.0%	62.5%	300 V
Touch-proximity	30.0%	40.0%	255 V

Closeness of authority figure

Milgram also decided to look at whether having the experimenter in the same room as the participant had an effect. To do this, Milgram got the authority figure to meet the participant but then leave the room and give the orders via a telephone.

Condition	Participants who gave 450 volts	Participants who gave 300 volts	Mean voltage given by the participants
Original	65.0%	100.0%	405 V
Order given over the telephone	20.5%	42.5%	270 V

Culture

Kagitcibasi (1996) examined parental attitudes to their children's behaviours across a wide range of nationalities. In certain countries, such as Turkey and Indonesia, it was expected that children were obedient to their parents with little room for independence. However, other countries such as USA and Korea were the opposite: independence was encouraged and unquestioning obedience discouraged.

Replications of Milgram

Country	Participants who went to 450 volts
Australia	68%
Italy	80%
Austria	85%

Some psychologists will use the individualistic–collectivist argument for obedience – cultures that are **individualistic** are theoretically less likely to be obedient compared to **collectivist** cultures.

The environment

Milgram's experiments that looked at the environment included:

- *Ordinary man*. In this study Milgram chose to have an ordinary man as the person giving the orders (authority figure). He was dressed in normal clothes (so no white laboratory coat).
- *Run-down building*. In this study Milgram changed the setting. He chose to run the experiment in a run-down commercial building in a shopping area.

Condition	Participants who gave 450 volts	Participants who gave 300 volts	Mean voltage given by the participants
Original	65.0%	100.0%	405 V
Ordinary man	20.5%	30.0%	240 V
Run-down building*	47.5%	62.5%	300 V

*It should be noted that here two participants refused to give even the lowest shock of 15 volts. This is the only variation on Milgram's experiment where some participants gave no shock whatsoever.

Description and evaluation of studies into social loafing

STUDY: LATANÉ, WILLIAMS AND HARKINS (1979)

Aim: To assess the role of social loafing in cheering and clapping behaviour.

Method: Male students were asked to clap or cheer as loudly as they could. They did this either alone, in a pair or in groups of four or six people.

Results: The amount of noise produced by the students decreased sharply as the number of students in the group increased. Therefore, there was a negative correlation between noise made and group size.

Conclusion: These findings support the idea of social loafing. This is because the group was putting less effort into cheering when there were more people around.

EVALUATION

● The task was quite artificial and may lack ecological validity.

✚ Because this was an experimental design, Latané et al. could be confident that it was the group size that affected the amount of social loafing that happened.

STUDY: ARTERBERRY, CAIN AND CHOPKO (2007)

Aim: To investigate whether social loafing exists when children are asked to solve problems.

Method: Participants were 192 5-year-old children in America. The children were randomly assigned to either working alone or in a pair. The children were then given either an easy or a hard puzzle, so there were four conditions:

1. Alone with easy puzzle.
2. Alone with hard puzzle.
3. In a pair with easy puzzle.
4. In a pair with hard puzzle.

For each of the four conditions, half were told that their work would be evaluated after completing the task, whilst the other half were not told this.

The hard puzzle was a 60-piece jigsaw of a bear outside a shop, where the outer border had already been completed. The easy puzzle was another jigsaw that was simply columns of different colours.

The experimenter recorded how many pieces of the puzzle were in the correct place after 5 minutes.

Results:

Mean number of pieces placed correctly within the first 5 minutes as a function of task difficulty (easy or hard puzzle), evaluation and working context (alone or with partner)				
	Alone		Paired	
	Evaluation	No evaluation	Evaluation	No evaluation
Hard puzzle	8.25	10.56	9.56	14.31
Easy puzzle	17.63	19.38	25.06	14.88

Conclusion: Social loafing only happened when the children were not going to be evaluated with the easy puzzle. This shows they were putting less effort into the task. However, this was reversed for all of the other conditions, which showed social facilitation (children helping each other out).

EVALUATION

➕ Arterberry et al. were confidently able to conclude that it was the type of puzzle and the group size that were affecting the amount of social loafing and social facilitation.

➖ The sample consisted of children from America, therefore the results may only be applicable to American children in terms of the level of social loafing seen.

Factors affecting social loafing

See p. 36 of *Psychology for GCSE Level, 2nd Edition*.

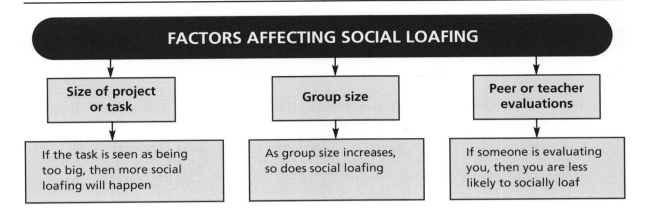

Description and evaluation of studies into deindividuation

STUDY: JOHNSON AND DOWNING (1979)

Aim: To investigate the effects of deindividuation on antisocial behaviour.

Method: The participants were 60 female students from a university in America. Participants were either dressed in robes with hoods or in a nurse's uniform. The conditions were:

1. Robes and hood with name tag.
2. Robes and hood without name tag.
3. Nurse with name tag.
4. Nurse without name tag.

There were 15 participants per condition. The participants were asked to decide the level of electric shock another person should get for failing to perform a task. To do this the participants were given a choice from +3 to –3, where +3 was to increase the shock to a high level and –3 was to decrease the shock to a much lower level. Before choosing, the participants saw the responses of a further three participants.

Results: When the participant was deindividuated (no name tag) the level of shock increased the most, particularly when the clothing was associated with antisocial behaviour (e.g. the robes and hood). See graph on p. 37 of *Psychology for GCSE Level, 2nd Edition.*

Conclusion: When a participant was deindividuated (e.g. no name tag present on photograph) they began to follow the "norm" of that group.

EVALUATION

- Johnson and Downing only used female American students as their sample. This may make it difficult to generalise to male behaviour or the behaviour of females outside of America.

- Ethical issues: Participants may have been placed under psychological stress. As no shocks were delivered they were also deceived.

- Johnson and Downing could be confident that it was the level of deindividuation affecting the level of antisocial behaviour.

STUDY: ZIMBARDO (1970)

Aim: Zimbardo wanted to test whether deindividuation makes people show more antisocial behaviour.

Method: He used groups of four female college students. They were asked to deliver electric shocks to another woman (they were fake though!). There were two conditions:

1. Each participant in the group dressed in a laboratory coat and hood immediately on arriving for the study. The room was dimly lit and no names were ever used. This was the deindividuation condition.
2. No hoods or coats were worn, the laboratory was brightly lit and all the participants wore clear name tags.

See photo of the experiment on p. 38 of *Psychology for GCSE Level, 2nd Edition*.

Results: As Zimbardo expected, the participants in the deindividuation condition gave out shocks for much longer compared to the other group.

Conclusion: The study shows that deindividuation does make people show more antisocial behaviour.

EVALUATION

- Zimbardo only used female American students as his sample. This may make it difficult to generalise to male behaviour or the behaviour of females outside of America.

- Ethical issues: Participants may have been placed under psychological stress as they believed they were giving shocks to a stranger. As no shocks were delivered they were also deceived.

- Zimbardo could be confident that it was the level of deindividuation affecting the level of antisocial behaviour.

Factors affecting deindividuation

See p. 39 of *Psychology for GCSE Level, 2nd Edition*.

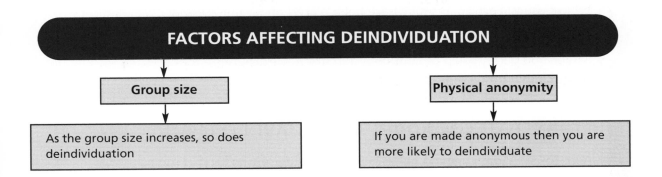

Description and evaluation of studies into bystander intervention

STUDY: LATANÉ AND DARLEY (1968)

Aim: To investigate whether being in a group affected reporting of an incident.

Method: The male student participants were sat in a small waiting room and then asked to complete a questionnaire. As soon as the participant had completed two pages of the questionnaire, the experimenter began to introduce smoke through a small vent in the wall. The time taken to report the smoke to the experimenter was noted. There were three groups who participated:

1. *The alone condition.* The participant was sat alone in the room ($n = 24$).
2. *The passive condition.* The participant was in the room with two confederates (fake participants) who did not react to the smoke ($n = 10$).
3. The group of three people in the room were all real participants ($n = 24$; eight groups of three).

Results: Participants were much less likely to report the smoke in the passive condition (10%) or when there were three real participants (38%). However, in the alone condition 75% of participants reported the smoke.

Conclusion: Being in a group affected the reporting of the incident. When other people were around, participants were *less* likely to report the smoke incident.

EVALUATION

○ Latané and Darley only used male students as their sample. This may make it difficult to generalise to female behaviour or the behaviour of females outside of America.

○ Ethical issues: Participants may have been placed under unnecessary psychological stress during the procedure.

○ Latané and Darley could be confident that it was the group size that affected the amount of bystander intervention that happened.

STUDY: PILIAVIN, RODIN AND PILIAVIN (1969)

Aim: To investigate helping behaviour in a real-life setting.

Method: The field experiment had a setting of an express train in a New York Subway. Four teams of students made up the research team. One played the victim, a second was a model and the other two were observers.

Around 4450 people on the train were the unknowing participants in the study over a period of 3 months. The train route selected meant that there was a period of 7.5 minutes when there were no stops. Seventy seconds into the journey, the victim staggered forward and collapsed. See the layout of the subway carriage on p. 43 of *Psychology for GCSE Level, 2nd Edition*.

The situation was varied in the following ways:

• Race of victim.
• Type of victim.
• Whether the model helped out.

Measures of helping behaviour were taken.

Results: Observers reported that there was more immediate help if the victim had a cane compared to when they were drunk (many more helped the cane victim within 70 seconds of the collapse).

The percentage of conditions where help was given was analysed by race of helper and race of victim; see graph on p. 43 of *Psychology for GCSE Level, 2nd Edition*. The table below shows the percentage of trials where the helping behaviour occurred, by type of victim.

	White victim – cane	White victim – drunk	Black victim – cane	Black victim – drunk
White helper	63%	91%	37%	9%
Black helper	75%	25%	25%	75%

Conclusion: An apparently ill person is more likely to receive help compared to someone who is drunk. The race of the victim has little effect on the race of the helper, except if the victim is drunk.

EVALUATION

➕ The study has ecological validity. That is, it was measuring the real-life bystander intervention of participants, showing what people will do in a real-life scenario involving someone requiring help.

➕ The sample size was very large, which means that there was a much higher chance that the sample had a wide range of people in it, making generalisation stronger.

➖ The study may be unethical. Participants could not give consent to take part in the study, and they were deceived because they would have believed the collapse was real. Finally, there is no way of assessing the psychological stress a participant was placed under.

➖ There may have been other factors that affected the likelihood that someone helped out that had nothing to do with the race or type of victim. This means that Piliavin *et al.* would be less confident that it was the type or race of victim affecting the amount of help behaviour.

STUDY: BATSON, O'QUIN, FULTZ, VANDERPLAS AND ISEN (1983)

Aim: In a series of three experiments, Batson *et al.* were interested in what motivates people to help others.

Method: The participants were 20 male and 20 female students from an introductory psychology course. They were randomly assigned to either the *easy* or *difficult* escape conditions (as highlighted below).

The participants were always placed in the role of the observer. They watched closed-circuit TV footage (a videotape) of a same-sex participant in the role of a worker. They watched them attempting to recall numbers. As they were recalling, the worker received mild electric shocks at random intervals.

In the *easy* escape condition, just before observing the worker, the real participant was given the following information: "*. . . although the worker will be competing two and ten trials, it will be necessary for you to observe* only the first two . . ." (p. 710). In the *difficult* escape condition, the participant was given differing information: "*. . . the worker will be completing between two and ten trials*, all of which you will observe . . ." (p. 710).

The real participants did not know that the worker would elect to do all 10 trials. However, after trial 2, the real participant had a chance to take the place of the worker.

Therefore, just after viewing the second trial, an experimenter appeared on screen asking the worker if he/she was OK. The worker hesitantly said yes and revealed that he/she had a traumatic experience with a shock in childhood. Hearing this, the experimenter comes up with the idea that the real participants could "trade places" with Elaine or Charlie. Twenty seconds later, the experimenter appeared to ask the real participant if he/she would replace the worker for the remaining trials. Prior to this the real participants had completed a questionnaire measuring their emotional response towards the worker's distress.

One final point to note: Participants were split into emotional response groups based on the questionnaire. They were classified as either *distress* or *empathy*. The *distress* participants were more likely to choose adjectives such as *upset*, *worried* and *alarmed* as their emotional response towards the worker. The *empathy* participants were more likely to choose *sympathetic*, *moved* and *compassionate*. Batson *et al.* wanted to see which of these groups was more likely to take the place of the worker.

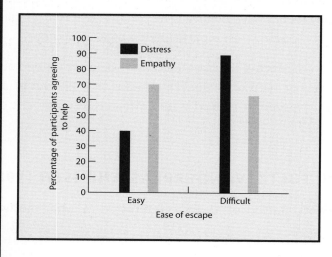

Results: As can be clearly seen from the graph, in the *easy* condition, the empathy group was much more likely to help and take part in more trials than the distress group. However, in the *difficult* condition, the distress group was more likely to help and take part in more trials than the empathy group.

Conclusion: People's motivation to help differs, depending on the scenario. If people are feeling compassionate or sympathetic then they are more likely to help out if the situation is perceived as being "an easy way to help". However, if the situation is seen as being difficult, then people who feel distressed and upset are more likely to help.

EVALUATION

➕ People were randomly assigned to groups so that it was less likely that participant variables got in the way of the independent variable.

➖ Low levels of ecological validity.

➖ Ethical issues: People may have been stressed by watching others in pain.

Schroeder, Penner, Dovidio and Piliavin (1995)

When will people help?

- People will help if they decide that something is wrong and that their help is needed.
- People will conduct a cost–benefit analysis. If the costs (money, too dangerous, not got the expertise) outweigh the benefits then no help is given.

What motivates people to offer help?

- People are more likely to help if they have had direct or indirect experiences of similar events.
- If we feel "connected" to the person in need then we are more likely to help them.

Are some people more helpful than others?

- In many cases of bystander intervention, men and women react differently. People tend to help in ways that are consistent with what is expected as a male or female.
- People who show high self-efficacy tend to help more – that is, people who believe that their attempts to help will be successful will help out more often.

Factors affecting bystander intervention

See pp. 47–48 of *Psychology for GCSE Level, 2nd Edition*.

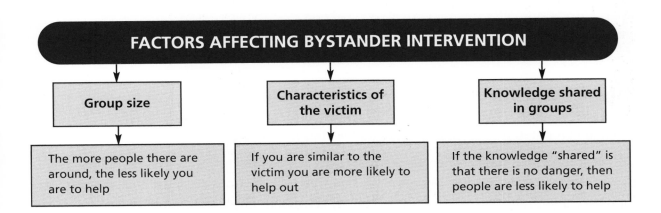

Contemporary practical application – keeping order in institutions

See pp. 48–49 of *Psychology for GCSE Level, 2nd Edition*.

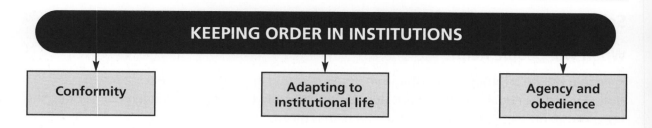

Conformity

The idea of normative conformity can be applied to prisons. Inmates may conform to the prison system because of a desire to be liked.

Adapting to institutional life (Goffman, 1961)

There are three phases:

1. In the *colonisation* phase, prisoners make themselves fully at home in the prison and do not want to leave. As a result, prisoners will go along with the demands of the prison for this to happen.
2. In the *conversion* phase, prisoners imitate the actions of staff and are used by them on various tasks. Therefore, when prisoners are in this phase they will follow the rules of the prison without question.
3. Finally, in the *playing it cool* phase, the prisoners may not be fully cooperative to rules and regulations but will follow them sufficiently to survive their stay in prison.

Agency and obedience

Milgram proposed that for a prisoner to do this they must have two social states:

1. An *autonomous* state – when we are free to act as we wish.
2. An *agentic* state – when we give up our free will in order to serve the interests of a wider group. In the case of prisons, this means going along with the orders of the prison guards to keep peace within the group of prisoners. So the prisoners are "agents" of those in authority and will do as they are told to ensure that the prison environment is a decent place to live.

OVER TO YOU

Now try the following revision activities:

1. Create spider diagrams *or* mind maps for all of the sections and flow charts entitled "Factors affecting . . .". Make sure you draw little pictures to remind yourself of the material.
2. For each of the studies you need to know, type up all the sentences separately for the aim, method, results and conclusion. Cut out each sentence and muddle them together for *all* the studies and try to put them *all* back in order. Good luck!
3. With the "Factors affecting . . ." sections in this chapter, use colour coding to help you revise. For each flow chart that highlights the different factors (e.g. those affecting conformity), colour in each factor in a different colour (e.g. for conformity use yellow for size of group, green for status of group members, etc.). As you then read the studies in the chapter, you can then colour code them as examples of each of the factors.

EXAMPLE EXAM QUESTIONS

1 Using an example, define the term *obedience*. **2 MARKS**

2 Describe **one** study into conformity and evaluate it in terms of one strength and one weakness. **6 MARKS**

3 Explain, using concepts from psychology, how we can keep order in institutions such as prisons. **6 MARKS**

4 Outline **two** factors that can affect bystander intervention. **4 MARKS**

MODEL ANSWER TO QUESTION 4

One factor is the size of the group. The larger the group, the less likely we are to help, as we think that someone else will do it instead. A second factor is the characteristics of the victim. For example, Piliavin showed that the white participants were much more likely to help out a white victim because they shared characteristics.

8

SEX AND GENDER

What's it about?

Biological psychology is an approach that emphasises the role of biological factors in the study of our behaviour. These include genetics, hormones, brain function and evolution. Therefore, our behaviours could be controlled by biological mechanisms. The topic of focus for this chapter is sex and gender. One debate is how much our *sense* of being a male or female is influenced by biological factors or by psychological factors such as upbringing, observation and cognitive processes.

WHAT'S IN THIS UNIT?

The specification lists the following things that you will need to be able to do for the examination:

- Outline definitions of sex identity and gender identity and the distinctions between them
- Describe biological differences between males and females (chromosomes and hormones)
- Outline and evaluate the psychodynamic theory of gender development, including Oedipus and Electra complexes
- Outline and evaluate the social learning theory of gender development, including imitation, modelling and vicarious reinforcement
- Outline and evaluate the gender schema theory of gender development

Key terms

Here is a list of important terms that you should learn in your revision. Try to write definitions for these after reading the chapter, and check your answers in the glossary on pp. 131–136. Essential terms that you *must* know in order to properly understand the topic are marked with an asterisk.

Castration anxiety	Introjection	Schema
Chromosomes	Libido	Sex identity*
Electra complex	Modelling	Testosterone
Gender identity*	Oedipus complex	Vicarious reinforcement
Hormones	Oestrogen	
Imitation	Penis envy	

The distinction between sex and gender

Sex identity

This term refers to the *biological* status of being a male or a female. This is based on chromosomes and genitals.

■ **Remember – when psychologists refer to *sex* they mean the *biological* status of a person.**

Gender identity

This term refers to the *psychological* status of being a male or a female. It includes an awareness of which gender you consider yourself.

■ Remember – when psychologists refer to *gender* they mean the *psychological* status of a person.

The role of chromosomes in typical gender development

Males	Females
XY chromosomes	XX chromosomes
Y from sperm	X from sperm
This dictates growth of sexual organs and testosterone	This dictates growth of sexual organs and oestrogen

It should be noted that it is the release of sex hormones at about 8 weeks into pregnancy that determines our biological sex. All embryos prior to this time are actually female and it is only the release of testosterone that makes the female sex organs develop into male sex organs.

The role of gonads and hormone production in typical gender development

We will look at the role of *two* hormones: **oestrogen** (females) and **testosterone** (males).

Males	Females
Testosterone	Oestrogen
Required for sperm production, the development of male reproductive organs Involved in the production of facial hair, the deepening of the voice and muscle growth	Required for sexual development, puberty, the stimulation of egg production and female reproductive organs
Produced in the testes and adrenal glands	Produced in the ovaries

Psychodynamic theory

- Freud believed that early experiences plus our unconscious mind help us to develop our sense of being a male or a female.
- Libido (sex drive) is with us from birth.
- The "energy" created has to be "used up" in socially appropriate ways.
- So, for the first year our libido is centred on our mouth (called the oral phase).
- This moves on to the anus (called the anal phase) as we get a bit older.
- By the age of 3–4 years it shifts to the penis in boys and clitoris in girls (the phallic stage). During this latter stage Freud believed that we develop our sense of gender.

Males	Females
Oedipus complex	Oedipus complex (sometimes referred to as Electra complex)
Boy's libido creates some sort of "desire" for the opposite-sex parent	Girl has the same unconscious desires for her father
Father may become angry if he finds out about this desire	But, she also fears the loss of her mother's love
The boy does not necessarily know this as it may happen in his unconscious	The girl does not necessarily know this as it may happen in her unconscious
Boy fears that his father will castrate him, causing castration anxiety	Noticing that her mother does not have a penis, the girl experiences penis envy
Gets rid of his anxieties by identifying with his father	She feels that she has already been castrated
Boy introjects the father's personality and adopts many gender roles attached to being a male	She then introjects her mother's personality and adopts many gender roles attached to being a female

EVALUATION

➕ Freud studied a boy called Little Hans who had a fear of horses, as they reminded him of his father. Once Hans had identified with his father by resolving the Oedipus conflict, the phobia disappeared and he began to act in a sex-typed way.

➖ As we are dealing with unconscious mechanisms, it is virtually impossible to test out the theory directly.

➖ There are alternative more plausible theories that can explain gender-appropriate behaviour, such as social learning theory and gender schema theory.

Social learning theory of gender

Remember the *ARRM* approach to social learning and the fact that we also **observe, imitate a role model** and may see **vicarious reinforcement**.

- **Attention**: The child pays attention to the same-sex parent's behaviours and attitudes.
- **Retention**: After observing the same-sex parent, the child retains the information for future use.
- **Reproduction**: The child has to be capable of reproducing the behaviour they paid attention to and retained. However, sometimes this can be very difficult to do (e.g. fixing a car or using an oven).
- **Motivation**: This can be both internal and external. Internal motivation can come from the child getting satisfaction from what they have done. External motivation can come from the child being reinforced for showing gender-appropriate behaviour. Remember that if the child observes their same-sex parent getting rewarded for gender-appropriate behaviour, then this is a third type of reinforcement called *vicarious reinforcement*.

EVALUATION

- ➕ Fagot and Leinbach (1989) reported that parents do encourage gender-appropriate behaviour in children as young as 2 years.

- ➕ Perry and Bussy (1979) demonstrated that children will even play with gender-neutral objects if a same-sex model does so beforehand.

- ➖ The theory cannot explain how some gender-appropriate behaviour is shown in children who have never observed that behaviour.

- ➖ The theory portrays children as being passive and easily manipulated by models. Children are quite active in their behaviour.

Gender schema theory

Schemas or schemata are pockets of information that people have about certain things in the world. Martin and Halverson (1987) thought that we have gender schemas to help us understand the complex nature of sex and gender. They are an organised set of beliefs about how each gender *should* behave:

- *Stage 1*: Initially children learn what things are associated with their own gender. This usually takes the form of toy choice, so boys play with toy guns and girls with dolls. Think about how some parents and even peers respond to a boy playing with a doll and dressing up in mother's shoes, or a girl playing with toy cars.
- *Stage 2*: A new type of schema begins to emerge at the age of 4 or 5 years old. The child begins to make links between existing schemas, to allow a more complex understanding of the world.

For example, children begin to think about what boys can do and what girls can do with toys, and how they behave.

- *Stage 3*: From around the age of 8 years the final schemas begin to emerge. The child begins to formulate new schemas based on the opposite sex, to get a more complete view of the world based on sex and gender. This is when children begin to think about what sorts of jobs men do and what sorts of jobs women do, and how they themselves would be viewed.

EVALUATION

🔁 Bradbard et al. (1986) assigned gender to gender-neutral objects and found that children spent more time playing with the "gender-appropriate" objects. This also happened a week later when the children were re-tested. The objects had fitted into their gender schemas!

⊖ Parents are important in the development of gender. Gender schema theory ignores this.

⊖ Some psychologists have noted that the theory does not explain why gender schemas develop in the way they do and why we need them to make sense of the world.

OVER TO YOU

Now try the following revision activities:

1. **Put all of the stages of psychosexual development for males and females (Oedipus and Electra complexes) on different post-it notes or index cards. Then, when complete, muddle the notes or cards together and then try to place them in the correct order.**
2. **Using index cards, write down all of the essential terms on one side and their definitions on the reverse. Get someone to test you on them.**

EXAMPLE EXAM QUESTIONS

1 Distinguish between sex identity and gender identity. **2 MARKS**

2 Describe and evaluate the psychodynamic theory of gender development. **6 MARKS**

3 Outline the gender schema theory of gender development. **4 MARKS**

4 Explain, using psychological theory, why Billy wants to be a mechanic when he is older. **5 MARKS**

MODEL ANSWER TO QUESTION 1

Sex refers to the biological aspects of a person, whereas gender refers to psychological aspects. So, sex is determined by genes and genitals, and gender is what the person thinks they are in terms of being male or female. Sometimes they do not match.

AGGRESSION

9

What's it about?

The word *aggression* is used a great deal in everyday language but a precise definition of an aggressive act is difficult to pin down and depends, to some extent, on opinion. Is a professional boxer aggressive? Is a tennis player aggressive when she throws down her racquet after missing an easy ball? One reason why aggression is difficult to define is that we need to look at the motivation behind an action, rather than the action itself, in order to make the judgement.

In this chapter we will consider three types of causes of aggressive behaviour: biological (Is it in our genes?), psychodynamic (Is it a manifestation of the unconscious mind?) and social learning (Is it the result of copying others?).

Many people believe that aggression is a problem in society and we will go on to consider the use to which these theories can be put in order to reduce aggression.

WHAT'S IN THIS UNIT?

The specification lists the following things that you will need to be able to do for the examination:

- Explain aggression in terms of the following:
  - ☐ Biological explanations, including the role of hormones, brain disease and chromosomal abnormalities
  - ☐ Psychodynamic explanations, including the frustration–aggression hypothesis
  - ☐ Social learning explanations, including modelling, punishment and monitoring
- Describe and evaluate studies of the development of aggressive behaviour
- Discuss ways of reducing aggression, based on these explanations
- Evaluate these ways of reducing aggression

Key terms

Here is a list of important terms that you should learn in your revision. Try to write definitions for these after reading the chapter, and check your answers in the glossary on pp. 131–136. Essential terms that you *must* know in order to properly understand the topic are marked with an asterisk.

Aggression*	Generalise	Sublimation
Catharsis	Id	Testosterone
Correlation	Longitudinal study	Vicarious punishment
Displacement	Monitoring	Vicarious reinforcement
Frustration–aggression hypothesis	Psychodynamic	
	Social learning theory	

Definition of aggression

We can define **aggression** as "the intention to inflict some form of harm upon others".

Explanations of aggression

Biological explanations

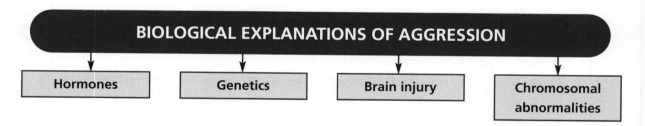

Hormones

Testosterone may be associated with aggression. Since adult males have higher levels of testosterone than adult females, this would account for why men are more aggressive than women.

Research evidence

- Experiments on mice show that aggression increases dramatically if they are injected with extra testosterone.
- Studies indicate that the testosterone levels of violent male criminals may be higher than those of the ordinary population (e.g. Kalat, 1998).

EVALUATION

➕ Research studies such as those cited indicate a link between levels of aggression and testosterone levels, especially ones showing that injections of extra testosterone increase aggression.

➖ Most studies show a correlation between levels of testosterone and levels of aggression. However, correlations do not show cause and effect, so these studies do not necessarily show that aggression is *caused* by high levels of testosterone.

➖ Studies on mice cannot necessarily be generalised to humans.

Genetics

The genes that people inherit result in different levels of aggression. In other words, some people are "naturally" more aggressive than others.

Research evidence

Cairns et al. (1990) interbred the most aggressive mice over 25 generations and found that each generation was progressively more aggressive.

EVALUATION

➕ Studies like that of Cairns et al. (1990) support the idea that there is an inbuilt genetic difference in levels of aggression, at least in mice.

➖ Evidence from studies of one species cannot necessarily be generalised to other species. In humans, our behaviour is very much influenced by socialisation, whereas behaviour in mice is comparatively little controlled by learning.

➖ Aggression may run in families due to learning and social learning rather than genetics.

Brain injury

Injuries to the brain, such as those caused by an accident, a stroke, a tumour or some conditions such as epilepsy, may cause an increase in aggression.

Research evidence

There are case studies that support this hypothesis. For example:

- Charles Whitman.
- Phineas Gage.

(See p. 83 of *Psychology for GCSE Level, 2nd Edition*).

The study by Raine et al. (1997) also provides support (see p. 286 of *Psychology for GCSE Level, 2nd Edition*).

EVALUATION

➕ There is a considerable body of biological evidence to indicate that brain injury can lead to an increase in aggression in certain cases.

➖ Case studies are, by definition, studies of single individuals and so every type of brain injury is unique. It is therefore difficult to generalise from these cases to all cases of brain injury, even if the injury is in a similar part of the brain.

Chromosomal abnormalities

The male abnormality XYY (normal is XY) may lead to aggressive behaviour.

Research evidence

There is a higher proportion of XYY in the prison population.

EVALUATION

➕ The research evidence of criminal populations in prison.

➖ There is evidence that the majority of XYY individuals are no more aggressive than XY.

➖ Most of the criminals with XYY have not committed violent crimes.

➖ Since we do not know how many of the general public have XYY, we do not know what percentage have committed crimes – it could be very low.

Psychodynamic explanations

Freud

- Freud believed that we are all born with a death instinct (thanatos) that becomes an aggressive instinct (part of the **id**).

- The *ego* tries to control the aggressive instinct by the use of defence mechanisms such as displacement and sublimation.
- Failure to control the aggressive instinct can result in unprovoked episodes of violence.

(See pp. 84–85 of *Psychology for GCSE Level, 2nd Edition*).

EVALUATION

➕ There are some case studies in which aggression (especially sudden bursts of aggression) could possibly be traced back to childhood experiences that correspond to Freud's theory.

➖ There is no way of proving conclusively that thanatos, the id, the ego and other constructs suggested by Freud actually exist.

➖ Freud's theories are untestable.

The frustration–aggression hypothesis

- Frustration *always* leads to aggression and *all* aggression is caused by frustration.
- A modified version of this original hypothesis is called the *arousal–aggression* hypothesis. This states that frustration leads to arousal, which often, but not always, leads to aggression.

EVALUATION

➖ Sometimes frustration leads to other feelings such as depression.

➖ Aggression can be triggered by factors other than frustration, such as being in a very noisy environment.

Social learning theory

According to this theory, aggression is learnt by observation and imitation of role models:

- Children observe and imitate important people in their lives (referred to as models). If parents are aggressive, then their children are likely to be. Other significant people are peers and role models from the media, so if children watch a lot of violent TV they are likely to be aggressive in the same way.
- A process called **monitoring** may increase or decrease the tendency of children to carry on behaving in the way they have learnt from their early role models. In *monitoring*, we look at our own behaviour. If we feel good about what we have done, this strengthens the behaviour and we are more likely to do it again.

- **Vicarious reinforcement** and **vicarious punishment** also influence children – see p. 87 of *Psychology for GCSE Level, 2nd Edition*.

EVALUATION

⊕ There is a considerable amount of experimental evidence and evidence from correlational studies to support this theory: for example, Bandura et al. (1961), Huesmann et al. (2003) and Klinesmith et al. (2006) – see pp. 87–92 of *Psychology for GCSE Level, 2nd Edition*, and below.

⊕ It explains why aggressive people often have aggressive parents.

⊖ The experimental studies lack ecological validity, so they do not necessarily reflect how people behave in everyday life.

⊖ The correlational studies do not necessarily show cause and effect – it is possible that naturally aggressive people seek out violent TV and films.

⊖ Social learning theory does not take account of the role of biology in causing individual differences in levels of aggression.

Studies of the development of aggression

STUDY: BANDURA, ROSS AND ROSS (1961)

Aim: To investigate whether young children will imitate an aggressive model.

Method: This was an experiment. There were four conditions:

- A group of girls and a group of boys who were exposed to a same-sex aggressive model.
- A group of boys and a group of girls who were exposed to an opposite-sex aggressive model.
- A group of girls and a group of boys who were exposed to a same-sex non-aggressive model.
- A group of boys and a group of girls who were exposed to an opposite-sex non-aggressive model.

The children each watched a model behaving aggressively or non-aggressively with a bobo doll and some Tinker toys. The study was carefully controlled: each child watched the same series of aggressive or non-aggressive actions alone with the model.

Results: Children in the aggressive condition reproduced a great many of the physical and verbal aggressive acts they had observed. In the non-aggressive condition, the children showed no aggression at all but simply played with the toys in a non-aggressive manner.

- *The effect of gender*: Boys reproduced more physical aggression than did the girls, but there was no difference in boys and girls with respect to verbal aggression.
- *The effect of the sex of the model compared with the child*: Boys were more likely to be aggressive if they had seen a male model rather than a female one, and girls were more likely to be aggressive if they had seen a female model rather than a male one.

Conclusion: The results show strong evidence that children are likely to copy new types of behaviour that they would have been unlikely to produce otherwise.

EVALUATION

➕ This study used an experimental design, with the children randomly split between aggressive and non-aggressive conditions, so it is reasonable to conclude that it was the aggressive model that caused the children to show aggressive behaviour rather than anything else.

➕ The findings have important implications for everyday life, since children watch a lot of aggressive behaviour on television and in films (and sometimes in real life).

➖ The experiment was carried out in artificial conditions (children are not usually left alone with a model who behaves in this way) so the study lacks ecological validity. This means it does not necessarily tell us much about the real-life behaviour of children and so we cannot be sure that the results **generalise** to real-life situations.

➖ There are ethical concerns with this study. Very young children were placed alone in an unfamiliar room with a stranger who acted in a very aggressive manner. They may have been upset by the whole procedure. They also learnt new ways to be aggressive.

STUDY: HUESMANN ET AL. (2003)

Aim: To see if there is any relationship between watching violent TV when young and violent behaviour in adult life.

Method: This was a **longitudinal study** that involved a **correlation**. It was a longitudinal study because they looked at the same group of people over 15 years. It involved a correlation because they looked for a relationship between the amount of media violence the people had watched and the amount of aggression they showed.

Results: The more violence a child watched, the more likely they were to become aggressive adults. In other words, there was a positive correlation between amount of violent media watched and aggression.

Conclusion: The amount of violence a person uses in adult life is related to the amount of violent media they experience during their childhood, not to how aggressive the children were at the start of the study.

EVALUATION

➕ This study has important implications for society. It is estimated that by the time a child is 18 years old he or she will witness on TV about 200,000 acts of violence, therefore it is very important that we study its effects.

➖ The problem with any correlation is that it does not necessarily show cause and effect – it does not automatically follow that watching violent TV or playing violent games *causes* people to be aggressive. It could simply be that aggressive people like watching violent TV programmes and playing violent video games.

STUDY: KLINESMITH ET AL. (2006)

Aim: There were two related aims:

1. To see if handling a gun increased testosterone levels.
2. To see if handling a gun increased aggression levels.

Method: Thirty male students (aged 18–22 years) were told that they were taking part in a study of taste sensitivity and their testosterone level was measured by using a sample of saliva. Each man was then given a gun or a toy and was asked to take it apart and put it together again according to instructions. Half the men had a pellet gun and the other half had a child's game. After 15 minutes, each man's testosterone level was measured again.

The men were then given a cup of water and a bottle of hot sauce. They were told that the water would be given to the next man in the study and they could put as much hot sauce in the water as they liked. This was used as a measure of aggression.

Results: Testosterone went up about 100 times more in the men who handled the gun than in those who handled the toy. On average, they put three times as much sauce in the water. In essence, the more a man's testosterone went up after the gun handling, the more aggressive he was using this measure.

Conclusion: The researchers concluded that these results suggest that guns may increase aggressiveness by increasing the level of testosterone.

EVALUATION

➕ As this is an experimental design with a control group, it does provide evidence that testosterone levels may be raised by certain situations that people associate with violence and aggression.

➕ This study may have important implications. Gun crime is a serious problem in the USA and in Britain. If handling a gun raises testosterone levels, then societies need to consider how wise it is for people to have easy access to guns.

➖ The sample size is not very large, nor is it representative as only college students were used. We cannot therefore assume that these findings would apply across the age range or to social groups other than students.

➖ The way of measuring aggression lacks ecological validity and therefore does not necessarily mean that these situations would result in more direct aggression.

Ways of reducing aggression

The psychodynamic approach – catharsis

Freud believed that a psychologically healthy way of controlling or reducing aggression is to release it by means of **catharsis**. This can be achieved by using indirect methods, such as by playing hard physical sport or watching a violent film.

EVALUATION

● One of the biggest problems with catharsis is that watching such things as violent films, a boxing match or real-life violence does not appear to reduce our aggressive urges. In fact, it tends to do the opposite and make us more violent. Social learning theory appears to be a better explanation for the way people respond to watching aggressive behaviour.

● There is much research which demonstrates that playing sport can increase aggression (e.g. Patterson, 1974; see p. 93 of *Psychology for GCSE Level, 2nd Edition*).

● Since there are instances in which people appear to need to express their aggression or it may "explode" in uncontrolled anger, it may be possible that Freud was partly right and that "safe" outlets are necessary.

The social learning approach

If significant models that children encounter in their everyday lives – parents, teachers, TV characters – acted in a non-violent manner then aggression could be significantly reduced.

It is important not to directly reward aggression and to discourage it as much as possible from as early an age as possible. Television could be used to emphasise the value of cooperation and non-violence rather than competition. With respect to video games, a challenge for the producers of these games is to provide exciting ones that do not centre around torture and killing.

It is also important to consider ways of reducing violence in already violent children. Such individuals need to be taught different ways of reacting to situations in which they are provoked. Role playing of potentially aggressive situations in order to teach non-violent responses has been a method used successfully by psychologists with violent young offenders.

EVALUATION

● Programmes using role play to teach young violent offenders non-aggressive ways of reacting to provocative situations have been partly successful. Quite often they reduce aggression in the young offenders' institute or prison but it is not clear how well they teach people to respond once they leave the institution and return to ordinary living (Ireland, 2000).

● There is evidence from many studies that children are liable to be more aggressive if they see a lot of aggression around them. This supports the view that violence could be reduced by reducing the level of violence that children see.

● Although reducing the amount of media violence that children experience is likely to reduce aggression, this can only ever be a partial solution. Children also need to have a stable, loving home in a culture that emphasises the importance of cooperation and caring.

OVER TO YOU

Now try the following revision activities:

1. Draw a set of flashcards for the three main studies in this chapter. On one side write the *Method used* and what they were trying to show (e.g. an experiment to study aggression; longitudinal correlational study of aggression), and on the other side write the name and date of the study. Test yourselves by looking at one side of the card (either side) and remembering what is on the other side.
2. Do a similar exercise, but this time the question side of the flashcard has the name(s) and date of the study and on the other side are the main findings.
3. Draw a series of cartoons to illustrate the development of aggression using the three sets of theories covered. Hence, the one for social learning theory could start with a child watching his mum hitting his sister and so on.

EXAMPLE EXAM QUESTIONS

1 Describe and evaluate the way in which social learning theory would suggest that aggression could be reduced (use continuous prose). **6 MARKS**

2 Outline an explanation of aggression based on the frustration–aggression hypothesis. **4 MARKS**

3 Describe **one** study of the development of aggression. **4 MARKS**

MODEL ANSWER TO QUESTION 3

Note that it is always best to include the aim, the method, the results (findings) and conclusion.

Huesmann et al. (2003) aimed to see if there was a relationship between the amount of violent TV that young people watched and how aggressive they were in later life. They carried out a longitudinal study, looking at the amount of violent TV a group of children watched and seeing how aggressive they were 15 years later. They found that the more violent the TV that was watched, the more likely the person was to be aggressive in adult life, as measured by such behaviour as hitting their children and committing crimes. They concluded that the amount of violence a person uses in adult life is related to how much media violence they are exposed to in childhood.

RESEARCH METHODS

10

What's it about?

This chapter covers all the research methods in psychology and the issues that arise from them. A lot of this you will have covered as you revised the other chapters; this should not be unfamiliar to you. In the exams for Units 1 and 2, questions on research methods will appear throughout all the sections, so be prepared for this.

Research methods: Unit 1

Experiments

An **experiment** involves the deliberate manipulation of one variable to measure its effect on another variable while keeping all other variables constant (as far as possible). The **independent variable (IV)** is the variable the psychologist deliberately manipulates, whereas the **dependent variable (DV)** is the variable that is measured to see if it has been affected by the IV (see activity on p. 306 of *Psychology for GCSE Level, 2nd Edition*, to make sure you understand these variables).

Extraneous (confounding) variables are any variables that might affect the findings and give us false results. The main things that need to be considered are:

- **Situational variables**: All aspects of the situation have to be kept the same.
- **Participant variables**: If two groups of participants are used, it is important to make sure they are as similar as possible – usually the same number of males and females in each group and the same age range.
- **Standardised procedures**: The same procedure should be followed for every participant.
- **Standardised instructions**: The same instructions should be given to every participant in a particular condition.

Types of experiments

Type of experiment	Description	Positive points	Negative points (limitations/problems)
Laboratory experiment	Experiments carried out in very tightly controlled surroundings, often with special equipment available	These are the only experiments that allow confident conclusions about cause and effect, due to the fact that the confounding variables can be controlled	The study may therefore lack ecological validity because it does not reflect ordinary behaviour. The results of the study do not necessarily tell us much about everyday behaviour
Field experiment	Experiments carried out in everyday surrounding but still with manipulation of the IV	Behaviour in a field experiment is far more natural than in a laboratory setting, so this has greater ecological validity – it tells us more about ordinary everyday behaviour	It is not possible to have such tight control over variables in the field, so we cannot be so confident of cause and effect; other factors could influence the DV
Natural experiment (quasi-experiment)	Studies that examine a natural situation in circumstances that cannot be manipulated. The IV occurs naturally; it is not manipulated	A natural experiment has very high ecological validity because it is looking at completely natural behaviour. The findings can therefore be generalised to everyday life	We cannot draw any definite conclusions about cause and effect because there are far too many uncontrolled variables

Design of experiments (participant designs)

Independent groups

Repeated measures

Matched pairs

Design	Description	Advantages	Disadvantages	Points to note
Independent groups design	Two or more separate groups of participants are used, one group in each condition of the IV	Can be used in cases where a repeated measures design cannot be used because the investigation requires separate groups, such as a comparison of men and women, young people and old people, urban and rural dwellers	There may be important differences between the groups of individuals to start with and these, rather than the IV, may be responsible for differences in results	Important to match the groups as a whole on important characteristics, especially those that might affect the DV. Alternatively, use random allocation of participants to each condition
Repeated measures design	The same The same participants are used in all conditions of the study	Controls for individual differences between participants (participant variables)	Introduces problems of **order effects**, i.e. **practice effects** and **fatigue/ boredom**	Usually needs counterbalancing to offset the problem of order effects
Matched pairs design	Participants in each condition are matched on a one-to-one basis	Controls somewhat for individual differences between participants	Matching individual participants into exact pairs is difficult and requires a large number of participants from which to select pairs	Often impractical but has been used with pairs of twins. Note that it involves matching on a *one-to-one* basis, not simply matching of groups

Target populations, samples and sampling methods

The target population is the whole population in whom a researcher is interested. The aim of a researcher is to select a **sample** from this target population and try to get a **representative sample**. The most common samples and sampling methods are as follows:

Type of sample	Description	Advantages	Limitations	Method of carrying out
Random sample	A sample in which every member of the target population has an equal chance of being selected	There is no guarantee that all of the people you have selected will be available or willing to take part in your study	Random samples are rare in psychology because it is difficult to have a complete list of the target population	Use a computer-generated list or draw names out of hat
Systematic sample	A sample obtained by selecting participants at fixed intervals from a list	This ensures that you have a certain number from each age group, for example, and thus have a reasonable chance of producing a representative sample	Not always easy to obtain a list of the whole target population	Choose every 10th person from a list of the target population
Opportunity sample	One that uses anyone who is available and willing to take part	Easy and practical	Highly likely to produce a biased sample	Ask family and friends to participate

Random sampling

Presenting results: Descriptive data

Measures of central tendency

- The *mean* is the sum of all the scores divided by the number of scores.
- The *median* is the middle number in a data set after you have placed them in rank order.
- The *mode* is the most frequent score.

Dealing with anomalous results

If there is one very unusual result this may distort the data. Such a score is *anomalous*. Neither the median nor the mode will be affected by this score and will give a fair representation of the results, but the mean will be considerably distorted by it. Therefore, when you have one anomalous result it is better not to use the mean as a measure of central tendency, but to use the median (and the mode if appropriate).

Measure of dispersion

It is useful to know the spread of the scores. The easiest way to do this is to use the *range*, which is the difference between the highest and lowest scores. So, in the set of scores 4, 5, 5, 7, 7, 8, 9, 12, the range is 8 (12 – 4).

The range is quick and easy to calculate but is distorted by an anomalous score.

Tables, charts and graphs

- *Tables* should be used to *summarise* data, so that whoever is reading it can make sense of the numbers. A table may show median scores of two groups of participants alongside the range.
- *Bar charts* should be used to *summarise* data that are already in separate groups (e.g. males/females). Therefore, when groups are separated out you use a bar chart to display the information.
- *Line graphs* are used when you are plotting data that are *continuous* along the bottom axis and you want to show a trend.

Research in natural and experimental settings

Remember:

- Research in experimental settings tends to have low ecological validity (it does not reflect real-world behaviour) but you can establish cause and effect (that the IV and nothing else has had an effect on the DV).
- Research in natural settings has high ecological validity (it reflects real-life behaviour) but you cannot control confounding variables, so you cannot be sure that only the IV and nothing else has affected the DV.

Ethics

Ethical guidelines are extremely important when conducting research.

Ethical issues	Ways of dealing with them
Deception: Participants should not be deceived unless it is absolutely necessary	Deception should be minimal and a full debrief explaining the need for deception should be offered
Consent: Wherever possible, the informed consent of the participant should be obtained	If this is impractical, a full debrief should be given
Confidentiality: Any personal information obtained in a study should be completely confidential	Participants must give permission beforehand if the researcher wants the results to be shared or published
Debriefing: Participants should, where possible, be debriefed	The participant should be informed of the true nature and purpose of the study at the end
Withdrawal from the investigation: It should be made clear to participants that they are free to withdraw from the investigation at any time	If participants look upset, the researcher should offer them the chance to withdraw
Protection of participants: Participants should not be placed under any great stress, nor should they be harmed, either physically or mentally	Stop a study if it looks as if the participants are under stress
The use of children: Young children cannot give consent, they may be easily upset and they may not be able to say that they do not want to do what the psychologist asks them to	• Gain the consent of the parent or guardian • Do not cause the children any upset or embarrassment • Stop the study if the child shows any reluctance to carry on

Writing an aim and hypothesis

Aim

The *aim* of a study is usually one sentence that clearly highlights what the researcher is intending to investigate.

Hypothesis

A *hypothesis* is a prediction. It is a sentence that states what the researcher predicts the findings could be.

An *alternative hypothesis* states that there will be a difference between two sets of scores, or a correlation between them (depending on the type of study that was done). It is a clear specific statement such as:

- Children who have watched an aggressive model will show a greater number of aggressive acts than children who have watched a non-aggressive model.
- There will be a relationship between reaction time and amount of alcohol drunk.
- There will be more words recalled from questions that ask about meaning compared to questions that ask about structure.

■ **Note that when writing a hypothesis, do this in terms of what is being measured, so it is very precise. Do not, for example, say that "children are more likely to be aggressive when watching an aggressive model compared to watching a non-aggressive model" because you have not said how the aggression is measured.**

Research methods: Unit 2

Note that when studying for Unit 2 you need to know all the research methods covered in Unit 1.

Methods of investigation

Experiments

For experiments, refer to the Unit 1 section.

Surveys

A **survey** is a means of collecting standardised information from a specific population (group of people), often using a questionnaire. In a survey, research information is collected from a sample of people who the researcher chooses in such a way that they are *representative* of the larger population.

EVALUATION

✪ Surveys can allow researchers to study large samples of people fairly easily.

✪ It is possible to generalise the results to a larger population.

⊖ It may be difficult to obtain a representative sample of the population.

⊖ People may not respond truthfully, either because they cannot remember or because they wish to present themselves in a socially acceptable manner.

Questionnaires

A **questionnaire** is a list of questions given to participants. They are used in surveys and are particularly useful when trying to investigate people's attitudes. The questionnaire may contain one of two types of questions:

- *Closed questions*: These have fixed alternative responses, such as: strongly agree, agree, uncertain, disagree, strongly disagree; or yes/no.
- *Open questions*: These give respondents the chance to express themselves more freely. For example: "Describe everything you can remember about your first day at school."

EVALUATION

Closed questions

⊕ Closed questions are quick to answer and score, and provide information that is useful in making comparisons – e.g. that 54% of people remember their first day at school.

⊖ They provide a very limited amount of information and leave no room for responses such as "it depends on . . .". They therefore lack validity (are not an accurate reflection of people's opinions).

Open questions

⊕ Open questions provide a source of rich and detailed information.

⊖ They take a lot longer to score and, since all responses are different, it is much more difficult to make comparisons between individuals or summarise data across groups.

Interviews

Structured interviews

A **structured interview** involves a list of questions that require the interviewee to choose from a selection of possible answers. It is basically a verbal means of presenting a questionnaire that has closed questions.

EVALUATION

⊕ It is easy to make comparisons between people because they all answer exactly the same questions.

⊖ You can only gain a limited amount of information, none of which is in-depth.

Unstructured interviews

An **unstructured interview** is a lengthier interview aimed at a detailed understanding of a person's mental processes. There are no set questions; the questions depend on the last answer given.

Observations

An **observation** involves watching people (or animals) and recording and analysing their behaviour. In order to carry out a good observational study the following things are necessary:

- For all observers involved in the same research operation to have a clear idea of exactly what they are observing.
- To use a system for categorising and recording behaviour.
- To use either a recording device (such as a video camera) or more than one observer.

Categories of behaviour in observations

The researcher has to decide on the categories of behaviour they are interested in. For example, for "aggression" it could be punching, kicking, hitting, verbal abuse and so on. For attachment it could be smiling at carer, moving towards carer, being upset when carer moves away, clinging to carer, looking at carer and so on.

Inter-observer reliability

It is important that observers looking at the same behaviour should categorise it in the same way. **Inter-observer reliability** is the extent to which there is agreement between observers. Inter-observer reliability is high if there is a considerable amount of agreement, but low if there is little agreement. Obviously a study that has low inter-observer reliability is a poor one. Observers should be trained in order to improve inter-observer reliability.

Types of observation

Type of observation	Description	Advantages	Limitations
Naturalistic observation	An observation of people in an everyday setting	High ecological validity, so the observations tell us a lot about everyday behaviour	It's not always easy for observers to remain completely inconspicuous, so it is possible they may affect the behaviour they are watching
Controlled (structured) observation	An observation carried out under conditions in which the researcher has some control, such as a laboratory or a specially designed room	All participants are in the same situation, so it is possible to generalise outside the group. You can also observe people in situations in which you may not find them in everyday life	May lack ecological validity because people are no longer in their natural environment, so their behaviour does not necessarily reflect that found in everyday life
Participant observation	The observers take an active part in the group or situation by becoming members of the group they are studying	The observer can gain much greater insight into the behaviour of the participants than if they remain an outsider	There are ethical problems; the confidentiality and privacy of individuals should be respected. Keeping a careful record of the behaviours can cause practical problems

Case studies

A **case study** is an in-depth (detailed) investigation of a single individual or a small group of individuals.

EVALUATION

➕ Case studies are useful for investigating the effects of unusual experiences such as deprivation, hospitalisation, or unusual educational experiences.

➖ Case studies only relate to one individual or small group and we cannot therefore generalise to others from the result.

➖ There is a danger that the psychologist who looks at a case study may get very involved and not be entirely unbiased.

Correlations

A correlational study involves taking lots of *pairs* of scores and seeing if there is a positive or negative relationship (a **correlation**) between them.

The direction of a correlation

- A **positive correlation** means that high values of one variable are associated with high values of the other.
- A **negative correlation** means that high values of one variable are associated with low values of the other.
- If there is *no* correlation between two variables they are said to be **uncorrelated**.

The strength of a correlation

Some correlations are strong, others are weak. For example, students who spend many hours a week reading novels tend to score highly on vocabulary tests; this is a strong positive correlation. Students who spend many hours a week reading novels tend to perform slightly better than average on science tests; this is a weak positive correlation.

Correlations can be represented in the form of a graph called a *scattergraph* (or scattergram), with a dot for each participant indicating where he or she falls on the two dimensions.

A positive correlation: The taller the player, the higher the score.

A negative correlation: The more time spent playing computer games, the less time spent studying.

EVALUATION

➕ Correlations are very useful for making predictions. If two variables are correlated, you can predict one from the other.

➖ Correlations only show that a relationship exists between two variables. They do NOT show that one *causes* the other. There could be a third factor that is causing both. See pp. 321–322 of *Psychology for GCSE Level, 2nd Edition*.

No correlation: Where there is no relationship, variables are uncorrelated.

Issues in evaluating research

When judging how valid the findings of research are, it is helpful to consider the following:

- *Demand characteristics*: This term refers to the situation that arises when a participant works out what the aim of the study is and then acts according to that, and not their true beliefs. This can reduce the validity of findings, as the participant is not being truthful in their answers and/or behaviour.

- *Observer effect*: This occurs when people or animals change their behaviour because they know they are being observed. This can reduce the validity of the findings, as participants are not acting as they normally would.
- *Social desirability*: This is when a participant wants to *look good* to the researchers and often occurs when people are answering questionnaires. This reduces the validity of the findings, as the participant is not reporting their true opinions.
- *Gender bias*: This can occur if there is a gender imbalance in a sample of participants. It means that results cannot be generalised to the sex that is under-represented.
- *Cultural bias*: This can come about if a task or study gives an unfair advantage to one culture over another. For example, early IQ tests had questions about American State Capitals or American Presidents. Participants who are not American may score lower as a result, which is unfair.
- *Experimenter bias*: This can come about in a variety of ways:
  1. The experimenter may give away too much information in the brief or standardised instructions, which causes demand characteristics in the participants.
  2. The experimenter's belief about what they are studying can affect the results of that study.
  3. How the experimenter interacts with the participant can affect motivation in the participant. For example, if the experimenter is not that friendly, then the participant may not try as hard as if they were friendly.

EXAMPLE EXAM QUESTIONS AND ANSWERS

1 A psychologist working in a young offenders' institution wanted to assess the effectiveness of two different anger management programmes, called "Control" and "Keep Calm". This is what she did:

- From the target population of all the offenders who had been on the anger management programmes, she randomly selected 10 participants who had been on "Control" and 10 who had been on "Keep Calm".

- A week after their programme ended, all participants were given a questionnaire asking them to assess whether they thought their anger management was better, worse or unchanged by the programme. In addition, they were asked questions about other aspects of their behaviour.

(a) Describe **one** way in which the psychologist could have chosen a random sample of participants who had been on the "Keep Calm" programme. **2 MARKS**

Answer: The psychologist could put all the names of the people on the "Keep Calm" programme into a container and draw out 10 names.

(b) Identify **one** advantage of random sampling. **1 MARK**

Answer: It is likely to give a representative sample.

(c) The following questions were on the questionnaire. In each case, say whether they were open or closed questions by ticking the relevant box: **2 MARKS**

(i) I feel less angry now than before I started the programme:

YES/NO
Open ☐   Closed ☐

(ii) Describe any changes in how you feel about the staff since going on the programme.

Open ☐   Closed ☐

Answer: (i) is a closed question and (ii) is an open question.

(d) Without using the examples given above, give **one** example of another closed question the psychologist could use. **2 MARKS**

Answer: "Compared to when I started the programme, fewer things make me fly off the handle." Circle the response that best applies to how you feel: Strongly agree/Agree/Disagree/Strongly disagree

(e) Without using the examples given above, give **one** example of another open question the psychologist could use. **2 MARKS**

Answer: "What do you think the programme was trying to achieve? In your opinion, has it succeeded?"

(f) (i) Outline **one** advantage of open questions. **2 MARKS**

Answer: An open question provides much more detail than a closed question and gives insight into attitudes and opinions.

(ii) Outline **one** advantage of closed questions. **2 MARKS**

Answer: A closed question allows for comparison between people and gives information on what percentage of people hold certain views.

(g) The psychologist found that in the group that took part in the "Keep Calm" programme:

- One participant said that their anger had increased.

- Four said they felt no different.

- Five said they felt less angry.

She converted these scores to percentages.

(i) What percentage felt less angry? **1 MARK**

(ii) What percentage felt their anger had increased? **1 MARK**

Answer: 50% felt less angry; 10% felt their anger had increased.

(h) Identify **one** disadvantage of using questionnaires in psychological research. **1 MARK**

Answer: People may not tell the truth.

(i) Identify **one** advantage of using questionnaires in psychological research. **1 MARK**

Answer: It is a quick and easy way of gaining the opinions of a relatively large number of people.

(j) The psychologist decides to carry out a case study on the young offender who was angrier than before the programme started. Identify **one** ethical issue the psychologist would have considered before carrying out the case study and how she would have dealt with it. **3 MARKS**

Answer: Confidentiality is an ethical issue. No data about the participant should be published without their consent and/or the consent of the appropriate authority who is in charge of the participant. It should also not be possible to identify the institution in which the participant is staying.

GLOSSARY

Aggression: any behavioural act designed to harm a living creature, such as hitting, shoving or throwing things, kicking, fighting or biting; or any verbal act that is intended to hurt someone by non-physical communication, such as shouting, swearing, name calling or saying nasty things about someone.

Anonymous: having no known name, source or identifying features. Used to maintain participants' confidentiality in psychological research.

Anterograde amnesia: the impaired ability to encode, retrieve or store information after the onset of amensia.

Antisocial personality disorder (APD): involves a disregard for the rights of others that has been going on since the person was 15 years of age or younger. Only people over the age of 18 years can be diagnosed with this disorder.

Authoritarian personality: according to Adorno, a person with this type of personality is intolerant of others with differing views, is dominating, is attracted to groups where there are strong leaders and respects higher authority figures. It is a personality type that predisposes people towards prejudiced attitudes.

Authority figure: someone who is regarded by others as having power over a situation or group, e.g. researchers in Milgram's obedience studies.

Autokinetic effect: perceiving a stationary point of light in the dark as moving. This is caused by constant eye movement that keeps your retina active and working.

Aversion therapy: a method of decreasing unwanted behaviours using the principle of associating a noxious stimulus with an already conditioned stimulus to produce a desired conditioned response.

Body language: a type of non-verbal communication involving posture, gestures and touch. It is the way we stand and walk, and the gestures we use to convey information.

Boredom: tedious tasks within research may make participants less likely to perform in ways that reflect accurate abilities.

Brain damage: in relation to memory, this refers to the physical deterioration of brain structures involved in memory storage.

Bystander intervention: is when people help others who are in need. For example, if someone tripped up in the street and their shopping went everywhere and you helped, this would be bystander intervention.

Case studies: detailed investigation of a single individual or a small group of individuals.

Castration anxiety: the Freudian concept that, during the phallic stage, boys fear castration by their father.

Catharsis: a psychodynamic principle that is simply an emotional release. The catharsis hypothesis maintains that aggressive urges are relieved by "releasing" aggressive energy, usually through action.

Chromosomes: strands of DNA that carry genetic information.

Collectivist: cultures that tend to emphasise teamwork or working as a complete family unit and place less emphasis on individuality and independence.

Conditioned response: the name given to a response to a stimulus that has already been learned.

Conditioned stimulus: the name given to the neutral stimulus after the association with the unconditioned stimulus has been conditioned.

Confederates: people who pretend to be participants in psychological research, but are in fact aware of the research aim and have been told how to respond by the researchers.

Conformity: adjusting one's behaviour or thinking to match those of other people or a group "standard".

Control group: a participant group that does not experience the IV being tested (e.g. the group that experiences silence).

Controlled (structured) observation: an observational research method carried out in conditions over which the researcher has some control, such as a laboratory or a specially designed room.

Correlation: a statistical indicator representing the strength of a relationship between two variables. Correlations do not show cause and effect, only that a relationship exists.

Counterbalance: used with the repeated measures design to overcome the problems of practice and order effects. Involves ensuring that each condition is equally likely to be used first and second by participants.

Covert observations: observations in which the observer remains hidden or at least blends in with the scenery so does not affect the behaviour of those being observed.

Cross-sectional studies: using groups of people of different age groups to examine changes over time.

Cue dependency: in order for memories to be retrieved efficiently, there must be specific similarities to the time when the information was encoded into memory. There are two types of cue dependency: "state" and "context".

Cultural norms: a set of beliefs about behaviour that are specific to a particular cultural group. Some cultural norms can be shared across different cultures.

Debriefing: after a participant has taken part in a study, the true aim is revealed to them. They are then thanked and asked if they have any questions.

Decay: fading of stored information in long-term memory (LTM). Although LTM is unlimited in capacity and duration, memories will fade if unused.

Defiance: a desire to resist the demands of authority and *not* do as one is told.

Deindividuation: refers to situations when a person, in a group, loses their sense of individuality or personal identity and personal responsibility for their actions.

Dependent variable (DV): an aspect of the participant's behaviour that is measured in the study.

Discrimination: when we produce a conditioned response to only *one* specific stimulus even if there are similar ones in the environment.

Discrimination (social): the practice of unequal treatment of individuals or groups based on arbitrary characteristics such as race, sex, ethnicity and cultural background.

Displacement (emotions): a Freudian mechanism in which feelings for one person (e.g. your mother) are transferred onto someone else (e.g. your lover).

Displacement (memory): loss of information from short-term memory based on the "first in, first out" concept.

DSM-IV: DSM is a classification system of mental disorders (the *Diagnostic and Statistical Manual of Mental Disorders*). DSM-IV is the fourth edition of this.

Duration: the amount of time material lasts for in different stores of memory.

Ecological validity: the degree to which the behaviours observed and recorded in a study reflect behaviours that actually occur in natural settings.

Electra complex: an ambiguous concept that aims to adapt the Oedipus complex for female children. According to this theory, penis envy leads girls to resent their mother, and resolution only occurs when girls identify with their mother. Freud did not use this term.

Encoding (input): the processing of information in such a way that it can be represented internally for memory storage.

Ethical guidelines: a standardised set of rules for researchers in psychology. Key ethical considerations include informed consent, right to withdraw, confidentiality (anonymity), debriefing and protection of participants.

Experiment: the deliberate manipulation of one variable to measure its effect on another variable, while trying to keep all other variables constant. This is the only method that allows us to draw conclusions about cause and effect.

Experimental group: the participant group that experiences the IV being tested (e.g. the group subjected to loud music).

Extinction: when the conditioned stimulus no longer produces the conditioned response. This could be because the conditioned stimulus has no longer been paired with the unconditioned stimulus.

Extraneous/confounding variables: any uncontrolled variable that might affect the results, therefore giving false information.

Extraversion: a personality trait that is characterised by more sociable and impulsive behaviours than those shown by introverts.

Eye contact: a form of non-verbal communication that provides feedback to others on our mood and personality, regulates the flow of conversation and expresses emotion to others.

Facial expression: one of the most important forms of non-verbal communication because it conveys emotion. The six most recognised facial expressions are surprise, fear, anger, disgust, happiness and sadness.

Fatigue: long tasks within research are tiring, which may make the task more difficult over time and therefore affect the results.

Field experiment: an experiment where participants are (unknowingly in some cases) observed in natural settings. The researchers can still manipulate variables and observe how people react to these manipulations.

Flooding: a method of treating phobias whereby the patient is exposed to direct contact with the feared stimulus. As the body cannot sustain high levels of arousal for long, fear quickly subsides and the stimulus–fear association is broken.

Frustration–aggression hypothesis: the idea that frustration always leads to aggression and that all aggression is caused by frustration.

F-Scale: a scale that measures nine personality characteristics as a means of determining a person's level of authoritarianism.

Gender identity: the psychological status of being a male or a female, including an awareness of which gender you consider yourself to be.

Generalisation: the production of a conditioned response to a stimulus that is *similar* to but not the same as the conditioned stimulus.

Generalise: refers to whether a result/finding can be applied to the whole population (e.g. all the people in the world).

Hierarchies: a method of outlining information in a structured way, beginning with general information and ending with specific information.

Hippocampus: a region of the brain linked to memory processing and storage.

Hormones: chemicals that are secreted into the bloodstream. A hormone is released from a gland and affects a target organ.

Id: the most primitive part of our personality that likes to have its own way and be satisfied immediately. For example, if you are on a diet, it is the little voice that keeps saying "I want cake".

Imagery: a memory technique that encodes information as pictures (e.g. illustrations of memory models).

Imitation: adopting the values, attitudes and/or behaviours associated with a significant person. This can be a parent, a popular peer or even a celebrity.

Independent groups design: research that uses two (or more) groups in order to make comparisons. Each group experiences only one level of the independent variable; the dependent variable remains constant.

Independent variable (IV): some aspect of the research situation that is manipulated by the researcher in order to observe whether a change occurs in another variable.

Individual differences: differences between people that are not specific to a given social category, such as sex, gender, ethnic group, etc.

Individualistic: cultures that tend to promote independence, including being self-reliant and "thinking for yourself".

Informed consent: always applies to research participants, and refers to written or verbal consent to take part after they are given information about what they will be asked to do.

In-group: the group to which a particular individual perceives him- or herself as belonging.

Inter-observer reliability: how much two or more independent observers agree on the ratings given by the researcher prior to analysis of results. It is high if there is considerable agreement, and low if there is little agreement.

Introjection: the Freudian concept of adopting the attributes, attitudes or qualities of a highly significant person into one's own persona.

Introversion: a personality trait that is characterised by less sociable and more cautious behaviours than those shown by extroverts.

Laboratory experiment: an experiment carried out in very tightly controlled surroundings (but not necessarily a laboratory), often with special equipment.

Law of Effect: the process by which if behaviour is followed by a pleasurable experience, the behaviour is more likely to be repeated. However, if the behaviour is followed by something not pleasurable, the behaviour is less likely to be repeated.

Libido: any "natural" drive. In sex and gender topics, this refers more specifically to the sex drive and is motivated by the pleasure principle.

Longitudinal study: when the same participants are studied over a number of years, even a lifetime, in order to study changes over time (e.g. the TV programme *Child of Our Time*).

Long-term memory (LTM): a relatively permanent store that has unlimited capacity and duration. Different kinds of LTM include episodic (memory for personal events), semantic (memory for facts) and procedural (memory for actions and skills).

Matched pairs design: research involving two participant groups that consist of pairs of individuals who are as similar as possible (often this is twins). Each pair is divided, and one of each is assigned to each group.

Method of loci: a memory technique of associating items to be learned with physical locations (e.g. remembering a shopping list by linking items to where they are in the supermarket).

Mind maps: free-ranging diagrams that use organisation and imagery to encode information so that it can be retrieved more easily.

Modelling: the act of watching a role model and then attempting to imitate what was just observed.

Monitoring: in monitoring, we look at our own behaviour. If we feel good about what we have done, this strengthens the behaviour and we are more likely to do it again.

Natural experiment: an experiment where researchers can take advantage of a natural situation in order to carry out an investigation in circumstances that they cannot themselves manipulate.

Naturalistic observation: observing behaviour in a natural, everyday situation, with observers remaining inconspicuous to prevent influence on the behaviour they are observing.

Negative correlation: a relationship in which as one variable decreases, the other one increases.

Negative punishment: the removal of something nice that decreases the probability of that behaviour being repeated.

Negative reinforcement: the removal of something aversive (unpleasant) that increases the probability of that behaviour being repeated.

Neuroticism: a personality trait that is characterised by anxious, depressed and tense behaviours.

Neutral stimulus: any stimulus that causes no response from the organism being conditioned.

Non-participant observation: any observation in which the observer remains separate from the people being observed.

Non-verbal communication (NVC): messages expressed by communication other than linguistic means.

Obedience: behaving in a certain way in response to the demands of an authority figure.

Observation: watching participants' reactions, responses or behaviours within psychological research.

Oedipus complex: the Freudian concept that, during the phallic stage, boys perceive their fathers as a rival for possession of their mother's love.

Oestrogen: the female sex hormone required for sexual development, puberty, the stimulation of egg production and female reproductive organs.

Opportunity sample: consists of participants selected because they are available, not because they are representative of a population.

Order effects: in repeated measures design, the order in which participants do the tasks can affect the results, because of practice, tiredness or boredom.

Organisation: a memory technique that encodes information in a specific way (e.g. always using a yellow sticker on cognitive psychology notes).

Out-group: the group to which a particular individual perceives him- or herself as not belonging.

Overt observation: observations in which the observers make themselves known to the people being observed (as would be the case for most participant observations).

Paralanguage: the non-verbal elements of communication that express emotion and the meaning of the message.

Paralinguistics: the study of *how* something is said rather than *what* is said.

Participant observation: an observational research method involving active participation within the study group or organisation by the researcher/observer.

Participant variables: possible confounding variables if participants are not as similar as possible, e.g. in age, sex or IQ.

Participants: people who actually participate in psychological research and are vital for research to be carried out. Used to be referred to as "subjects", but this term is no longer in use.

Penis envy: a Freudian concept that occurs when a girl realises she does not have a penis. Argued to be a defining moment in the development of gender and sexual identity for women.

Personal space: an invisible space around us that we allow people to whom we are close to enter, but if someone else comes into it we feel uncomfortable.

Personality: a relatively stable set of behaviours, thoughts and feelings that a person shows to others. It could also be a distinctive set of traits and characteristics that a person has.

Phonemic processing: processing things in relation to how they sound.

Positive correlation: a relationship in which as one variable increases, so does the other one.

Positive punishment: the addition of something aversive that decreases the probability of that behaviour being repeated.

Positive reinforcement: the addition of something nice (e.g. reward) that increases the probability of that behaviour being repeated.

Postural echo: a type of non-verbal communication in which people are seen to "mirror" the postures of a partner they are communicating with.

Practice effects: problems associated with participants repeating tasks within research, which may make the task easier for them over time and therefore affect the results.

Prejudice: an attitude that predisposes us to think, feel, perceive and act in favourable or unfavourable ways towards a group or its individual members.

Primary reinforcer: a reinforcer that fulfils a biological need directly (e.g. food fulfils hunger).

Proactive interference: when information that you have already processed interferes with new information you are trying to process, with the end result that you forget the new information.

Protection of participants: an ethical guideline stating that researchers must protect participants against psychological and physical harm.

Psychodynamic: the relationships between the mind and personality and mental or emotional consequences, especially at the unconscious level.

Psychoticism: a personality trait that is characterised by aggressive, egocentric and cold behaviours.

Quasi-experiment: any experiment in which the researcher is unable to manipulate or control variables, therefore not considered to be a "true" experiment.

Questionnaire: a set of questions dealing with any topic. Questions can limit responses (e.g. Are you male or female?) or be open-ended (e.g. Describe your childhood).

Random sample: consists of participants selected on some random basis (e.g. numbers out of a hat). Every member of the population has an equal chance of being selected.

Reciprocal inhibition: when you cannot experience two competing emotions at the same time (e.g. fear and relaxation).

Rehearsal: repetition of information in short-term memory to allow encoding into long-term memory (e.g. repeating a phone number in your head).

Repeated measures design: a research design where the same participants are used for all conditions in the experiment.

Representative sample: a sample that is chosen to be typical of the population from which it is drawn.

Retrieval (output): the ability to get information from our memory system in order to use it.

Retroactive interference: when new learning interferes with material that you have previously processed and stored.

Retrograde amnesia: the impaired ability to retrieve information acquired before the onset of amnesia.

Right to withdraw: an ethical guideline stating that participants can leave the study at any time without penalty, and their data will be destroyed.

Sample: the participants actually used in a study, drawn from some larger population.

Schema: an internalised mental representation that contains all the information, experience, ideas and memories that an individual has about an object or a sequence of events.

Secondary reinforcer: a reinforcer that can be exchanged for a primary reinforcer (e.g. money or tokens).

Semantic processing: processing things in relation to what they mean.

Sensory buffer: the first mechanism in Atkinson and Shiffrin's (1972) multistore model of memory. It picks up information that is attended to and sends it to short-term memory.

Sex differences: differences between people based on their biological sex.

Sex identity: the biological status of being a male or a female.

Short-term memory (STM): a temporary place for storing information, during which time it receives limited processing (e.g. verbal rehearsal). STM has very limited capacity and short duration, unless the information in it is maintained through rehearsal.

Situational variables: any aspects of the situation that might affect the findings, such as the room, the time of day, the lighting, etc. These must be kept the same for all participants.

Social learning theory: the theory that behaviour is learned by observation and imitation of others. Social behaviour is also influenced, according to this theory, by being rewarded and/ or punished.

Social loafing: situations where a person is likely to put in *less* effort in a group task.

Spontaneous recovery: after extinction, in the presence of the conditioned stimulus, the conditioned response suddenly reappears.

Standardised instructions: the experimenter must give the same instructions to every participant in any one condition.

Standardised procedures: the same procedures are used on every trial of an experiment to ensure that no confounding variables affect the dependent variable.

Status: level of social standing on a hierarchical scale. For example, an employer has higher status than an employee.

Stereotyping: the use of a stereotype towards an individual or group of individuals who share common traits (culture, race, religion, etc.). Stereotyping is an oversimplification, leading to positive and negative evaluations.

Storage: the memory system's ability to keep information that we can then use again if necessary.

Structural processing: processing things in relation to the way they look (e.g. the structure of things).

Structured interview: a list of questions requiring the interviewee to choose from a selection of possible answers.

Sublimation: a Freudian defence mechanism in which socially unacceptable impulses (e.g. aggression towards your father) are converted into socially acceptable impulses (e.g. playing football).

Survey: a research method that allows participants to self-report, via questionnaire or interview, their attitudes/feelings.

Systematic desensitisation: a method of treating phobias, whereby relaxation skills are associated with increasingly phobia-associated stimuli. It works on the principle that relaxation and fear cannot be experienced at the same time.

Systematic sample: consists of participants chosen by a modified version of random sampling in which the participants are selected in a quasi-random way (e.g. every 100th name from a population list).

Target population: the whole group to which a researcher wishes to generalise the findings.

Temperament: your *natural* disposition in terms of personality traits. That is, it refers to the personality you are apparently born with.

Testosterone: the male sex hormone required for sperm production and the development of male reproductive organs.

Token Economy: a method of behaviour shaping that rewards appropriate (desired) behaviours with secondary reinforcers (tokens) that can be collected and exchanged for primary reinforcers (something that is wanted).

Unconditioned response: the natural response to an unconditioned stimulus.

Unconditioned stimulus: a stimulus that elicits an involuntary bodily response all on its own, such as dogs dribbling at the sight of food.

Uncorrelated: there is no relationship between two variables, e.g. exam grades and height.

Unstructured interview: an interview beginning with a single question, from which further questions depend on the interviewee's answer.

Verbal communication: involves speech, and can also involve writing since this stands for language.

Vicarious punishment: learning by watching other people being punished rather than being punished directly.

Vicarious reinforcement: learning by watching other people being rewarded rather than being rewarded directly.

Volunteer sample: consists of participants who volunteer to take part in a research study, for instance by replying to an advertisement.

Going on to study
AS-Level Psychology?

If you are following the AQA–A specification, this is the ideal book for you:

AS LEVEL PSYCHOLOGY
FOURTH EDITION
by Michael W. Eysenck

"This excellent new edition of a successful and popular textbook, substantially rewritten, is full of new details, new studies and ideas, all directly relevant to the new specification. Many topics have been updated with current research and new examples and the style is accessible and friendly. There are also very useful online resources to engage students, plus some for teacher use. This is a valuable contribution to the teaching and learning of AS Psychology."

Evie Bentley, Advanced Skills Practitioner for Psychology, West Sussex Adult and Community Learning; Chairperson 1999–2002, The Association for the Teaching of Psychology

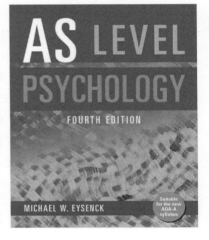

This thoroughly updated, full-colour, fourth edition of *AS Level Psychology* has a new focus on the nature and scope of psychology as a science with an emphasis on how science works, and guidance on how to engage students in practical, scientific research activities.

The book includes coverage of six key areas in psychology: Human memory, early social development, research methods, stress, social influence, and abnormality. Chapters focus on the application of knowledge and understanding of the text to help students develop skills of analysis, evaluation, and critical thinking. The book is packed with advice on exam technique and hints and tips on how to pick up marks, giving students the best chance possible of the highest grades. However, unlike other A-Level textbooks ,which focus solely on passing the exam, *AS Level Psychology, fourth edition* is also designed to foster an interest in the study of psychology as a subject with an additional general chapter to introduce the theories and explanations that make psychology a fascinating discipline.

AS Level Psychology, fourth edition is supported by our extensive resource package, *AS Level Psychology Online*. This is available free of charge to qualifying adopters of our A-Level textbooks. Student resources include the AS Level Psychology Workbook, multiple-choice quizzes, animations and interactive exercises, relevant podcasts with key figures in psychology and more. We also provide teacher resources, which include a week-by-week teaching plan, sample essays, chapter-by-chapter lecture presentations, and classroom exercises and activities.

Ψ Psychology Press
Taylor & Francis Group

ISBN 978-1-84169-711-6
£14.99 pbk
Published by Psychology Press

Please visit http://www.a-levelpsychology.co.uk/aqaa for further information.